Y0-BCU-873

The Future of Golf

The
FUTURE
of
GOLF

HOW GOLF LOST ITS WAY *and* **HOW TO GET IT BACK**

GEOFF SHACKELFORD

SASQUATCH BOOKS
SEATTLE

Copyright ©2005 by Geoff Shackelford
Pages 228–229 constitute an extension of this copyright page.
All rights reserved. No portion of this book may be reproduced or utilized in any
form, or by any electronic, mechanical, or other means without the prior written
permission of the publisher.

Originally published as *The Future of Golf in America: How Golf Lost Its Way in the
21st Century and How to Get It Back*, iUniverse, Inc., 2004
Revised edition, Sasquatch Books, 2005

Printed in Canada
Published by Sasquatch Books
Distributed by Publishers Group West
10 09 08 07 06 05   8 7 6 5 4 3 2 1

Book Design: Stewart A. Williams
Cover: ©Allen Kennedy/CORBIS

Library of Congress Cataloging-in-Publication Data

Shackelford, Geoff.
The future of golf : how golf lost its way and how to get it
back / Geoff Shackelford.
    p. cm.
ISBN 1-57061-456-3
  1. Golf--United States. I. Title.

GV981.S43 2005
796.352--dc22

                                        2004066289

Sasquatch Books
119 South Main Street, Suite 400
Seattle, WA 98104
206/467-4300
www.sasquatchbooks.com
custserv@sasquatchbooks.com

For everyone who has devoted their life to golf,
and to those who value its future.

"I have no wish to criticize anything, or anyone unfairly, but I believe that the only way to promote the interests of golf as a competitive sport is to discuss openly and fairly the problems which arise in playing the game."

—BOBBY JONES

"What a farce is this business of length? Golf is surely the only game, either in the United States or Britain, whose whole character has been changed solely by so-called 'improvements' in instruments in which it is played. I cannot believe that the parties concerned would alter the stands at Wimbledon, Forest Hills, Wembley, and Yankee Stadium simply to accommodate a new ball, which when struck in the same manner, happened to go further. I rather fancy they would tell the manufacturers what to do with their new ball."

—HENRY LONGHURST, 1953

"The very soul of golf shrieks!"

—CHARLES BLAIR MACDONALD

CONTENTS

Contents

FOREWORD

I am a great admirer of Geoff Shackelford's writing for two reasons. Firstly, I enjoy the lively, interesting way he writes on the varied golfing subjects he covers—I have a number of his previous books and they have a habit of finding their way onto my bedside table. Secondly, I like Geoff's work because he isn't afraid to say what he thinks. In an age where people are all too keen to sit on the fence or play it safe and say what they sense is appropriate or what they perceive people want to hear, Geoff tells it as he sees it. And of course, it helps that I happen to agree with about 95 percent of what Geoff has to say. Any more than 95 percent and I'd be guilty of one of those aforementioned modern afflictions!

In *The Future of Golf*, Geoff Shackelford pulls no punches. He fervently believes that the game he loves is in danger of being "crushed"; that it is "less fun" than it used to be, and is in danger of being "overrun by selfish business interests." In essence, Geoff's contention (or charge) is that the supposed custodians of the game have dithered when confronted with rapid, significant advances in technology and in so doing have meekly surrendered control to the all-powerful equipment manufacturers—whose motivation is seemingly singular and short-sighted. No doubt there are some who consider Geoff's views reactionary and think him some kind of a golfing romantic; personally, I think he is a realist, and I applaud his determination to speak out and encourage others to take action—ASAP.

The '96 Masters and my head-to-head duel with Greg Norman doesn't really feel that long ago to me, and yet golf has changed dramatically in the intervening years. Whenever I was asked to explain what I thought made golf such a special game I would mention the words "balance" and "strategy": no other sport, I would claim, so evenly rewarded power and finesse; no other game demanded precision one moment and encouraged imaginative play the next; and none other was capable of rewarding boldness and subtlety in such equal measure. Above all, the element that defined and distinguished golf was its emphasis on strategy. "It's like a giant, physical game of chess," I would say, "played outdoors on an ever-changing stage." I'm not sure I can make this claim anymore.

Today golf has become—or is in severe danger of becoming—a game disproportionately dominated by power and power players. The negative impacts and repercussions of this situation are legion, and they are eloquently described in this book. The effect on golf course architecture, a particular passion of Geoff's (and mine), for instance, is immense: Many, indeed most, of our classic courses are staring obsolescence in the face. Do we want to play (never mind have the time to play) 8,000-yard courses in the near future?

But it isn't all bad news. In addition to highlighting many of the game's most pressing challenges, *The Future of Golf* offers some innovative solutions to the current situation; and it concludes on a rather optimistic, upbeat note. Maybe Geoff is a golfing romantic after all?

—*Nick Faldo*, FEBRUARY 2005

PREFACE FOR THE NEW EDITION

"Time ripens all things."

—CERVANTES, *Don Quixote*

Millions watched the 2004 U.S. Open and wondered why the storied Shinnecock Hills links descended from a brilliant test of skill to a browned-out inspired freak show. Surpassing even the 1999 British Open antics at overcooked Carnoustie, the Shinnecock course setup debacle started Saturday when most well-struck balls rolled up to the hole, only to curl back off the severe seventh green. United States Golf Association (USGA) officials claimed that the green had been mistakenly rolled, an erroneous tale that would soon be recanted.

After howling overnight winds further dried out the course, Saturday's seventh hole antics spread to the entire layout for Sunday's finale. Hose-wielding crews were dispatched to cool down several baked-out greens. Conditions became so extreme, several players later predicted that a normal Southampton afternoon breeze might have forced an unprecedented suspension of final round play to unplayable conditions.

Thomas Boswell in the *Washington Post* labeled that final round "a day of almost hallucinatory golf embarrassments."

Golfweek's James Achenbach insisted that the event went sour because "contemporary golf is out of balance." He recommended "Mickey Mouse be named vice president of the USGA. The president? Goofy, of course."

The 2004 U.S. Open was more than just a tough course setup gone haywire. It exposed a much deeper ongoing saga that has been quietly debated, but largely misunderstood. After Shinnecock Hills, the struggle over golf's future was no longer a secret.

"They've lost the war with equipment," Tom Kite said, arguing that the extreme setup on a 6,946-yard course was the USGA's "only defense right now" in a sport where technology has rendered most courses obsolete and drastically changed its overall character.

This book was self-published in February 2004 to shine a light on the various issues that led to the Shinnecock Hills disaster. The story remains the same: Golf has been hijacked by corporate interests while its primary regulatory body, the USGA, resorts to extreme antics to mask their failure to uphold the most important tradition in this wonderful sport: the relationship between player and equipment.

If the golfer's equipment becomes as important as skill, then this valued cultural asset will not only be severely damaged, but it also will have been transformed into a commercially driven vehicle in pursuit of the latest consumable. The actual sport will be secondary to commerce.

Several sections of this book have been updated, including four additional essays inspired by recent incidents. Numerous sidebars serve as updates to the many topics covered. An epilogue also has been added to include comments from the prominent voices who are demanding that golf's regulatory bodies take back the sport from corporateers who believe golf exists merely to support their bottom line.

People who play golf are not consumers, they're golfers. And treated as golfers, they will support the commercial sector. But if regarded only as consumers existing to sustain quarterly earnings, they will ultimately reject the sport.

The separation between commerce and culture has all but vanished. This is the story of how it happened, and how we can reclaim the values that make golf the greatest game of all.

—Geoff Shackelford

ACKNOWLEDGMENTS

Saundra Sheffer, thank you for editing this manuscript and as always, offering sage advice. Ken Bakst, Ben Crenshaw, Jim Haight, Gil Hanse, Frank Hannigan, Mike Miller, David Moriarty, Ron Papell, Tom Paul, Diane Shackelford, Lynn Shackelford, Jim Wagner, Tim Weiman, Daniel Wexler, and Jon Winokur offered excellent suggestions and guidance, as did Tommy Naccarato, who designed the first edition cover in honor of George Thomas's *Golf Architecture in America*. Thanks to all of you for your continued support.

Thanks to Terence Maikels and the gang at Sasquatch Books for giving this book a chance and for your efforts in producing this edition.

To the many fine editors who gave me the opportunity to write the columns and stories reproduced here, thanks for your wisdom and editing touch: Larry Aylward, Pat Jones, and Frank Andorka at *Golfdom*; Mike James, Dave Morgan, and Randy Harvey at the *Los Angeles Times*; Geoff Russell and Mary Rung at *Golf World*; Dave Gould, Brad King, Tom Dellner, and R. J. Cerame at *Links*; Tara Gravel and Jim Frank at *Golf*; finally, Chris Millard, Stu Schneider, John Marvel, Dan King, Stuart Hall, Alex Micelli, and surely others I'm forgetting.

Many thanks to all of those who helped flesh out the more complicated issues, particularly several thoughtful past USGA presidents who continue to give back to the sport in their own unique ways. And finally, thanks to Google for making research so much easier.

INTRODUCTION

Something strange has happened to golf. The sporting pastime most associated with tradition, integrity, and artistry was quietly bestowed to business interests without the slightest concern for the future of golf. This book will explain how the sport has been taken over by cutthroat equipment sellers with assistance from a cowering United States Golf Association and a passive PGA Tour that refuses to learn from the demise of tennis.

Matters have been made worse by astronomic course construction costs and management companies trying to live up to Wall Street standards. This has added excessive expense while subtracting fun and value from the golfing equation.

Many thoughtful players, course architects, and writers have struggled to make their voices heard above the cacophony of advertising that trumpets "progressive" developments in equipment, golf architecture, course management, and maintenance practices.

Golfers, interested mainly in shaving a stroke off their scores or getting another 10-yard tee-shot boost, responded for a while with open checkbooks, unaware that the equipment choices they made were rapidly changing the sport.

Golf has spent the last 60 years subtly expanding and modifying its greatest asset, the course, to accommodate technology and the perception that buying distance-boosting equipment is the sport's ultimate source of pleasure.

But, our courses are like rubber bands. They are being stretched. The more they expand, the more they narrow. And we all know what happens to rubber bands when stretched too far. They snap.

Would baseball redesign its last few old ballparks and alter the diamond to accommodate a new (illegal) "hot" baseball? Would rich club owners or cash-starved parks departments across America tolerate the costly expansion of stadiums and Little League fields, just so Rawlings could market something "new"? Of course not.

Yet this is the concession golf had made at the expense of its future well-being. Since 1995, when companies started making solid core balls with softer covers, golf has witnessed drastic changes in the way it is played at the professional level. And starting around 2001, when companies were shown by the USGA how to get around testing procedures by optimizing player launch conditions, we've seen unprecedented distance increases on the PGA Tour.

This "progress" has been hailed as the savior of a struggling golf business. So the sport now tiptoes around common sense, merely to appease a handful of equipment manufacturers whose sole interest is to maximize profit margins, not to make golf a better sport.

Why has the USGA—whose job it is to regulate in a way that balances the role of equipment to keep existing courses relevant and costs from skyrocketing—seemingly stood pat as the sport flew by its timeless layouts on a collision course with 8,000 yards, 6-hour rounds, and $150 green fees? Actually, they didn't stand pat. The USGA advocated changing courses instead of regulating equipment.

Recent regimes of the organization ignored the advice of past presidents and key staff members, compromising golf by shelving ball-testing procedures that would have decelerated the equipment-fueled distance race, and thus, dispelled the myth that genuine golfing fun is derived from equipment consumption.

Golf has been deregulated. And now the future of the sport is in question.

It took some time and personal experience before I began to put the pieces of this puzzle together. The USGA had long made minor suggestions to U.S. Open courses, but when they started suggesting significant changes to the old courses that hosted or wanted to host the U.S. Open, it became apparent there was more to this story.

Many of the design alterations were poorly veiled excuses to battle increasing driving distances. In 2000, I wrote to USGA Executive Director David Fay and expressed my concerns about one course in particular, Riviera Country Club, which wants to host a U.S. Open. Fay denied that the USGA made any design suggestions. After all, if the folks who are supposed to govern the rules and protect the traditions of golf were suggesting alterations to compensate for changes in equipment occurring under their watch, such a scenario might not reflect well on the USGA, would it? Fay wisely wrote back that his organization never would demand changes to such revered courses and reiterated his love for Riviera's brilliant design.

A little more than a year later I learned that suggestions from the USGA staff and select executive committee members were implemented on more than one classic course. I also obtained a memo detailing USGA staff and executive committee member-suggested changes slated for Riviera. None involved genuine design restoration or improving everyday enjoyment of the course. So I wrote to Fay again.

Fay is the man who stood up to Ely Callaway during a live Golf Channel showdown back in 1998, where he explained why the USGA had to draw the line on springlike-effect drivers. That night, Fay eloquently stated the sure-to-be-unpopular case against allowing distance increases and why it was silly to ask golf's venues to accommodate a new and more marketable piece of golf equipment.

I figured Fay must have known that changing a time-tested classic course would not be popular or a good example for the tradition-proud USGA to set, right?

Fay wrote back and graciously allowed that everyone is entitled to their own opinion. Or in twenty-first centuryspeak, that means "bugger off and mind your own business."

I knew then that not only had the USGA lost control of the sport, but also they were aware of it and hoped to mask their complacency by altering U.S. Open venues. So, as player tee shots reached almost 400 yards at the 2003 U.S. Open, both Fay and USGA President Reed MacKenzie faced the NBC cameras and maintained, with straight faces, that they were "comfortable" with the way things were going.

Distance increases are a "natural evolution of a healthy sport," Fay said in another interview.

Little did I know that the USGA created a golf ball test that would have prevented the most recent distance surge, which has little to do with player athleticism and everything to do with companies using the USGA's own research to optimize launch conditions. That USGA–developed research led to a test that would have put them in control of the sport. However, the test formerly known as "optimization," was shelved in favor of one that will not stop this "progress," but instead works around the perceived needs of the marketplace and allows for more innovation that will do little to make golf more affordable, more fun, or more interesting for the average player.

The USGA will say this is flat-out wrong. Their new "Phase II" test should put an end to the distance race and restore order. But if that was so, they would not also be considering new language in their rule book that allows a tournament committee to set its own local rule requiring players to use a regulated competition ball. Such a move means the USGA is aware that it has let things go too far and needs a way out.

Regardless of who is at fault, the repercussions remain golf's most important issue. We are hiding our courses in unnecessary rough, trees, new back tees, and other superfluities that fail to improve the sport.

We have been told technology is golf's savior, but as we've seen amazing clubs and balls introduced, the sport has not grown nor does its future appear bright.

No, we do not need to go back to hickory shafts or discourage innovation of better clubs within the rules. Control of golf should not have been handed over to the manufacturers who have little interest—long or short term—in the sport's history, tradition, playing characteristics, or future. Their aim is immediate gain and maximum profit margin. And boy, are they profiting—at the expense of tradition and affection poured into this great sport by early stewards like Old Tom Morris, C. B. Macdonald, and Bobby Jones.

The good news is that the future of golf can still be a prosperous one. The ingredients exist to save the sport by returning to a few common-sense values that emphasize fun over consumerism. But first, golfers have to understand what went wrong and what has to happen for golf to have a healthy future.

PART I

WHAT'S UP WITH GOLF . . . IN A BIG NUTSHELL

"If it works, it's obsolete."

—Marshall McLuhan

The sport formerly known as golf was once arguably the most complete of all leisure and professional pursuits. It was rich in character thanks to visionaries who crafted unique courses while adopting sound rules governing the sport. Playing golf required strategic planning to succeed. People of all ages and physiques enjoyed it. Golf was humorous and idiosyncratic. It worked.

But to assuage the "free market," many cherished traditions have been crushed. Golf has transmogrified into a bizarre shadow of its former self, immersed almost overnight in doublespeak and an infomercial-like attitude that continues to obscure meaningful discussion of the sport's rich history and tradition.

Ah, but you say, all is well! Tiger is here. Golf is cool. Didn't you see the limited edition lithograph of Old Tom Morris on the wall? We celebrate tradition here!

Actually, tradition has been auctioned off in the name of the marketplace. Golf is in serious danger of becoming just like too many other pastimes—controlled by a select few with only dollar signs in their hearts and minds. That perhaps would be tolerable if the sport was attracting new players, affordable for everyday golfers, and preserving its most hallowed grounds.

Instead, the golf business is in serious trouble because golfers are playing less, or not at all. There is no mystery why play is down: excessive cost, excessive time required, and excessive difficulty.

As my friend Tim Weiman says, golfers want to "play more, not pay more!"

AN OVERVIEW

"The governors of the game have a responsibility to govern the game and the governors have not been doing so."
—FRANK "SANDY" TATUM, FORMER USGA PRESIDENT

The governing bodies have shrugged off most traditions because of ignorance or the lure of money. Neither reason reflects well on them. Yes, they conveniently cling to certain traditions when they want to tell us what strong "core values" they have, and they deflect skeptics by serving up fog-filtered images of golfing inner-city kids to remind us that charity is their true mission in life.

During the late 1990s, the United States Golf Association—governors of golf in North America—amassed a small fortune through wise investments and massive U.S. Open revenues. A sizeable nest egg was built, presumably to suggest that they were financially able to battle hawkish equipment manufacturers who threaten a lawsuit whenever the game's legal guardians suggest overdue regulation.

Yet, it should be noted that the companies did not file suit when, in 2003, the USGA announced a "Phase II" change in golf ball testing that purportedly put a cap on the golf ball. This was not because the equipment companies had become kinder and gentler. No, they understood that the same convenient loopholes exist in the *new* USGA ball test as were present in the old test. (More on the ball test in Part II.)

The PGA Tour is becoming a big bore, thanks in large part to an overdose of bland architecture that fails to elicit passionate play. Course setups lack imagination, either providing us with over-rigged fairway contours and hole locations to keep scoring in line with that peculiar modern notion of "protecting par." Or, tournaments reflect the other extreme, excessive birdie shootouts where drama is just as rare and players partake in a contest to see who makes the most putts while announcers spend most of their time reminding us how great everything is.

Rarely is there that classic balance between a course vulnerable to great play, while penalizing the player who mismanages the design. In the tour's defense, constant and often unbelievable increases in distance make the balance between risk and reward nearly impossible to present.

Meanwhile, big-name players are marketed instead of the sport, leading to a NASCAR–like atmosphere in which shotmaking and architecture take a back seat to product plugs, the occasional celebrity scandal, and often-embarrassing youth worship.

This degeneration occurred even though the PGA Tour has a megawhopper of an example of how *not* to expand an audience: professional tennis. Once a great sport, the power-emphasis version of modern tennis has become unbearable to watch for more than a few minutes, a situation stifling pro and recreational tennis.

"Players with these high-tech racquets are able to hit every stroke as hard as they can. I find it a little monotonous."

—Bud Collins, noted tennis analyst

Tennis's mistakes are obvious. Force over finesse. Technology over common sense. Celebrity over sport. Youth over universal appeal. And it's all neatly packaged under the progress banner.

Still, you may ask, how does this affect my game at Bethpage or Riverside or Griffith Park? Here's how. When pro tennis chose power over all-around shotmaking, it killed enthusiasm for the sport. Amateur tennis participation levels dropped from 34 million players to 13 million in less than fifteen years. Bigger graphite racquets did not make tennis more fun to play or watch, but did make it easier to bash away at the ball.

Golf is now a manufacturer-driven power game and the numbers are stagnant. The sport is not growing, nor has it really grown that much since the 1950s, despite what the marketing folks claim.

And here's the sad part: Tennis didn't even change its courts! Service boxes did not shrink to combat faster serves like golf narrowed its fairways. Baselines weren't pushed farther away to allow players to swing away. In tennis, they simply changed the way their sport is played by failing to regulate equipment.

In golf, our precious venues are changed for the *worse* to deal with the power game. Instead of wide, fun, strategic, and forgiving designs that all players can enjoy while still testing better golfers, our courses employ rough, length, and other tactics to transform gracefully conceived designs into grounds of discipline to punish tee shots that have the audacity to stray from the center line. This change came about as a result of years of rulemaking complacency, while the aforementioned trends accelerated in the twenty-first century by an accidental deregulation of golf.

With the arrival of Tiger Woods in the '90s and the resulting attention he attracted, there was an opportunity to foster the universally accessible sport that turn-of-the-twentieth-century Americans envisioned when they imported golf from Scotland. Thanks to Tiger, golf became popular and "cool." It had a chance to become a community sport that families and friends could enjoy together.

Affordable. Relaxing. Congenial.

Perish the thought!

Imagine a scenario in which a family goes to the neighborhood layout for a friendly game, shares a few laughs, and gets some exercise. The family dog trots along when junior and dad go to play on a summer evening. Shotmaking is an art form. Courses fit into their native environments. And a round can be played in 3 hours because the designs are not built to suit the power game.

That was the golf our great-grandfathers tried to hand down to us. Gradually, we've drifted from that model. But the sport is so good that the drift did not prove lethal.

There's little chance of the old golf model coming back in the U.S. even though it still thrives in Scotland as it has for a few hundred years now. Why not? Because the affordable family scenario doesn't fit into today's course-management company "business model." Of course, neither does the "upscale daily fee" model. Nor any other corporate management model.

Sure, millions still play regularly and love golf. Millions more are fans of the sport. But new golf fans are not familiar with the once-strategic, more intelligent version of the sport. And as indicated by the 2003–04 television ratings decline, the par-protecting tournament setup approach is beginning to stifle enthusiasm.

PGA Tour commissioner Tim Finchem dreams that golf might become as popular to watch on television as the NFL. People laugh at his dream. But, the sport was once on a path to becoming more universally popular with excellent long-term prospects. It was a scenario in which interesting courses would reward a variety of shotmakers, thus producing more dramatic tournaments every week. It was a scenario where people would watch because they could relate to the professional golfer's tribulations, while witnessing humans engage in these exciting battles over a compelling landscape. And, it was a scenario where we left the telecast feeling good when a talented player overcame obstacles in heroic fashion.

An inspiring pro game influences participation in recreational golf, which is why problems on the professional level are important to understand and address if we hope to improve everyday golf. The current version of modern pro golf is typically played on sanitized courses where the player who makes the fewest mistakes wins. The who-self-destructs-last concept may work for auto racing, but in golf it is downright boring to watch and certainly isn't any fun to play.

Taken to an extreme at major championships, we watch courses beat up on players in the name of par. That reminds viewers of the miserable version they know all too well. Some say they like seeing tour players experiencing the same pain they do. But the television ratings don't back that up. Who really wants to watch players sidestep land mines? Who cheers when someone taps in for par? I suppose the people setting up the courses like it because high scores boost their egos.

More importantly, who wants to play this negative version of golf when there is a positive, more enjoyable alternative just waiting to be rediscovered?

"It's no secret our industry is struggling. In my opinion the economy will turn around, weather will get better, and we'll still be talking about rounds being flat."

—M. G. ORENDER, PGA OF AMERICA PRESIDENT, FALL 2003

Golf course professionals, general managers, and superintendents will tell you that the ingredients are in place for a major slowdown in the business, if not a total collapse. Golf has ignored the warning signs and fallen prey to consumerism as its savior, instead of focusing on ways to enhance fun and preserve value.

By now you'd think it should have been apparent that golf's salvation lies not in buying a new $500 driver and playing a "country club for a day," but in the intrinsic richness of the sport itself.

By making distance the vital component of the golfer's arsenal, the USGA—those self-proclaimed "legal guardians of the game"—endorse a commercial version of golf in which the player must buy the latest ball and driver or else feel left behind. They've even rubber stamped manufacturer talking points that preach easier-to-use equipment as the way to grow the sport. Yet the USGA also points out that handicaps haven't gone down much with the advent of high-tech equipment. So if the latest and greatest clubs don't make the game easier for avid golfers, how will such equipment help beginners?

This contradiction is the result of a regulatory body running scared from the folks it should be regulating, fearful of being branded anti-free market or anticapitalist.

Golf equipment has traditionally provided tools for players to demonstrate their talent to craft shots for the situations they confront. Any hint of equipment compensating for skill has traditionally inspired regulation.

Meanwhile, the courses labeled "traditional" survive because they call upon intelligence, rewarding skillful play and shrewd thinkers. These courses do not exist merely to thwart improved equipment, nor were they created to provide a playground for the consumer to constantly test out new purchases.

"The penal school of golf spells death to that spirit of independence, life and freedom which we are all seeking, and which we should find of all places in our recreations."

—MAX BEHR, GOLF ARCHITECT

Penal design and the disciplinary mind-set all too often replace courses created to excite our senses the way the old links of Scotland still manage to do. Rough, bunkers, length, and other technology-combating elements only increase misery and expense while reducing opportunities to demonstrate creativity. Worst of all, penal designs force golfers to spend too much time on the course.

So the golfer pays handsomely. Twice. First for this week's must-have equipment, and then for the expense of maintaining all of the things needed to offset "progress": at least 150 acres of expensive-to-maintain land cluttered with features deemed necessary to combat driving distances incompatible with the design.

Oh, and the greens had better be lightning fast, but soft enough to hold these hot flying balls that golfers can't stop with their high-tech equipment!

The future depends on the existence of enjoyable, reasonably priced courses that offer a good value and can be played in a reasonable amount of time. Yet this notion is so rarely discussed in golf publications that golfers must wonder if they are bizarre for having such expectations.

"The print and electronic media have promoted a technophobic agenda since the start of the season, featuring such tabloid-ready headlines as 'The Weapons Race,' 'Ban This Ball or Els,' 'Going the Distance with Souped-Up Golf Balls,' and 'Cooling Hot Drivers.' The 24-hour Golf Channel contributes to the hysteria by allowing selected talent to spew one-sided antitechnology commentary and conduct 'leading-the-witness' interviews."

—WALLY UIHLEIN, CEO OF ACUSHNET (TITLEIST),
SPORTS ILLUSTRATED, JULY 2003

Why doesn't someone point out the insanity of changing complicated, large-scale venues in order to preserve the manufacturer bottom lines?

Wally Uihlein would like us to believe that the media have spewed "one-sided antitechnology commentary." But coverage has been minimal and typically protechnology, particularly when it comes to magazine reviews of new products.

Why are dissenting views rarely heard? Because certain manufacturers have threatened to pull their big advertising campaigns from golf magazines if they question the merits of technology-induced changes.

Titleist temporarily yanked a multimillion-dollar campaign in 1998 when a magazine editor and its very famous contributing editor wrote that golf needed a competition ball.

Certain television announcers make the problem worse, perpetuating manufacturer myths. What's more, several of these commentators also have lucrative endorsement deals on top of their network contracts. Jim Nantz of CBS does voice-overs for those clever Titleist ads poking fun at architects who want to preserve tradition and the integrity of the sport. And Titleist "design consultant" Peter Kostis has often repeated company talking points. Scores have not changed much, therefore, nothing is wrong!

As Phil Mickelson prepared to wallop a Titleist driver at the "Battle of the Bridges," Titleist staffer and then–ABC commentator Curtis Strange told viewers that he was against regulated equipment. The "great thing" about golf, according to Strange, is that we can go out tomorrow and buy the same driver that Phil is using right now. You could almost hear Titleist's Uihlein cheering his employee on: "You go Curtis! You tell 'em to shop till they drop!"

"For all of the ways technology has failed to improve the quality of life, please press three."

—ALICE KAHN

During the late 1990s, the classic golf course restoration movement kicked into gear. Several great old designs were dusted off and returned to their original glory, making golf more fun for the people who played these old gems. The movement even spread to a few public facilities, while more classic muni's designed by the likes of Tillinghast and Ross await, eager to be refurbished so that they can bring renewed joy to millions of devoted regulars.

In the recent technology boom, classic course owners and green committees have stopped restoring once-wide fairways and have decided not to enlarge their shrunken greens. Good players (who traditionally have more say) fear a course might become too easy after such restoration work. Instead, they look for ways to find length, add rough, narrow corridors, and, in general, add misery!

New courses are built to absurd lengths that few can enjoy no matter how many sets of tees are constructed. Typically these courses are built on properties unsuited for golf. They are created *not* with fun in mind, but to be "challenging" and to showcase high-flying target golf that few can handle.

Who wants to play a course that dictates shots most of us don't even have in our bags? Judging by the rounds played, fewer people every day.

Yes, better athletes on the tour also have helped to increase distance a bit. But don't forget, previous generations had people like Frank Stranahan and George Bayer, who arguably were bigger and stronger than anyone on the tour today.

And no, it's not just the ball and driver combination that has increased distance. Instruction is better, practice facilities are incredible, and innovative shafts allow people to swing harder than ever before. There is no denying the instant gratification that comes from buying a new club and gaining a few more yards off the tee. But the enjoyment is fleeting. When your playing partners buy the same clubs, your distance increase becomes a matter of relativity.

Initially, most golfers resist a distance rollback of the golf ball or a restricted competition ball. When you understand that sound, enjoyable architecture within everyone's reach keeps golfers coming back, you'll understand why we need to put a stop to the manufacturer-driven distance race.

Controlling the golf ball is the easiest solution for everyone involved and will reduce corporate control over golf. Instead of existing merely as a marketplace, golf will return to its place as a cultural asset. When that happens, the marketplace will thrive thanks to an enthusiastic customer base.

Besides pointing out the dangers of reacting to technology, this book addresses the architectural elements proven timeless while examining recent design trends that were born out of a response to "progress."

The issues addressed in this book are not new; they were debated more than 80 years ago. The critics then were fearful of the predicament we have now: a sport that has sold its soul to equipment manufacturers at the expense of fun and affordability.

Ah, but you say, the game has grown from around 3.5 million players in 1950 to around 26 million today. How can I gripe? Well, that frequently cited number is misleading. The 3.5 million represented the number of "avid golfers" in the then-U.S. population of 150 million. Today's 26 million includes folks who call themselves golfers but only have to play one round a year to count. There are around 5.9 million people today in a nation of nearly 291 million who say they are "avid golfers."

tra·di·tion—*A set of customs and usages viewed as a coherent body of precedents influencing the present.*

There is good news. The sport has survived threats to its integrity and it can do so again. All it takes is a little knowledge and an understanding of certain traditions that have demonstrated a tendency to survive.

And, yes, there are bigger issues in the world than adulterated golf. Peace, family, jobs, and health are all more important. But one joy of being a golfer or a fan of the sport is that you are a part of something royal and ancient. Golf is intelligent and multifaceted. Golfers enjoy debating issues concerning the betterment and preservation of the sport. No other sport produces such rich and interesting debate.

Golfers welcome new forums, a fact demonstrated by the vigorous activity of Internet golf discussion groups. And they clearly still embrace the traditional and want to be part of the beloved, time-tested traditions. Otherwise, they wouldn't make pilgrimages to hard-to-reach places like St. Andrews.

The purpose of this book is to help golfers get back in touch with the sport's roots, while hopefully providing a few laughs along the way. The recent disregard of golf's traditions has spiraled so far out of control that sometimes all you can do is chuckle! Ruefully, of course.

Now, if you believe it's best to shrug off these issues and let the "marketplace" sort things out, this book isn't for you. But if you seek a different future for golf and want to gain more insight into the past and present, these pages may help.

If we are unable to protect golf's greatest traditions and fail to pass along a healthy version of this singular sport to the next generation, then nothing is immune from compromise.

We can reclaim golf with a common sense approach to the rules, traditions, architecture, and the basic elements that make the sport affordable and fun. As the old saying goes, "everybody does better when everybody does better."

So guess what? Corporate golf will benefit too, if they would only listen and embrace certain fundamentals vital to golf's past and its future.

THE STATE OF GOLF INDEX

(with apologies to the Harper's Index)

Consumer spending on golf balls, clubs, and soft goods (gloves, shoes, bags) in 2002: $4.5 billion

Consumer spending on green fees, dues, initiation fees, and food and beverage in 2002: $16 billion

Annual spending in the American golf-course maintenance industry, including labor, product purchases, and other expenses: $9 billion

Percentage increase of additional land that the American Society of Golf Course Architects (ASGCA) estimates is necessary to accommodate safety and design of longer courses: 10%

Amount the ASGCA says this additional land and accompanying costs raises green fees: 17%

Number of courses owned by golf equipment manufacturers: 1

Average in-season green fee of *Golf Magazine*'s "Top 100 You Can Play" in 2004: $191.40

Number of courses under $100 in the "Top 30 You Can Play": 1

Number of courses under $100 in the "Top 100 You Can Play": 17

Percentage of PGA Tour players surveyed in 2003 by *Sports Illustrated* who said that limits should be imposed on golf balls to reduce distance: 60%

Percentage of superintendents in a 2004 survey who said maintenance of their course changed to compensate for the increasing distance of golf balls: 28%

Percentage who said so in a 2003 survey: 18%

Number of rounds played in the United States in 2000: 518.4 million

Number of rounds played in the United States in 2002: 502.4 million

Number of rounds played annually that Golf 20/20 initiative hopes the sport will reach by 2020: 1 billion

2002 estimate of the number of golfers who played at least one round per year in the United States: 26.2 million

Total number of golfers that the Golf 20/20 growth initiative hopes to create by 2020: 55 million

Estimated number of 250 million nongolfers in the United States "very or extremely" interested in taking up golf in 1998: 41 million

Estimated number of 265 million nongolfers in the United States "very or extremely" interested in taking up golf in 2003: 10 million

Average annual number of gallons of water used to maintain the typical eighteen-hole course: 18 million

Average annual number of gallons of water needed for each of the 113 desert golf courses in the greater Palm Springs area: 26.5 million

Average acreage of turf per course for golf courses in California, Arizona, New Mexico, Oregon, and Washington: 110 acres

Acres of turf on the eighteen-hole Greg Norman Course at PGA West in La Quinta, CA: 50 acres

Percentage of water used at the Greg Norman Course at PGA West compared to other desert courses: 50%

Average acreage of maintained turf for an eighteen-hole American course: 75 acres

Average annual golf course maintenance budget for an eighteen-hole American course: $584,500

Average annual golf course maintenance budget for an "upscale" 18-hole, 7,000-yard course: $1.2 million

Number of fairway residential lots in the United States created from 1998 to 2003: 300,000

Number of fairway residential lots in the United States sold from 1998 to 2003: 95,000

2002 number of regulation 18-hole courses (over 5,200 yards with a par over 66) in the United States: 13,876

2002 number of executive (shorter length and par range from 58 to 66) golf facilities in the United States: 897

2002 number of par 3-only golf facilities in the United States: 691 (out of 15,464 total facilities)

Number of golf facilities in the United States converted to housing or other real estate purposes in 2002: 50

Projected cost of the 9-hole par-3 and accompanying Tiger Woods learning center to be added to the "Dad" Miller Golf Course in Anaheim, CA: $25 million

Cost to build the 18-hole course and clubhouse for Rustic Canyon, *Golf Digest*'s "Best New Affordable Course" for 2002: $5 million

Number of new participants in a 1999 study by the National Golf Foundation that golf was attracting each year: 2.9 million

Number of participants in a 1999 study by the National Golf Foundation that golf was losing each year: 3.4 million

U.S. golfers in 2003 who are male: 76%

U.S. golfers in 2003 who are female: 24%

U.S. participants who call themselves occasional golfers, meaning those who play one to seven rounds per year: 55%

U.S. participants who call themselves moderate golfers, meaning those who play eight to twenty-four rounds per year: 22%

U.S. participants who call themselves serious golfers, meaning those who play twenty-five or more rounds per year: 23%

Number of "serious" bowlers in 1969: 9.5 million

Number of "serious" bowlers in 1999 after years of advances such as improved surface treatments that supposedly made bowling more enjoyable and accessible: 3 million

Tennis player participation in 1975 with wood rackets and shotmaking: 34 million

Tennis player participation today with high-tech, oversize rackets:
13 million

Number of kids, ages 5–17, participating in golf in 2001: 4.4 million

Number of kids, ages 5–17, participating in golf in 2003: 6.1 million

Percentage of the 16,000 American golf courses constructed from 1998 to 2000: 7%

Number of courses for sale as of this printing for prices sharply under their construction costs or recent sale prices: 400

(Sources: National Golf Foundation, Golf Research Group, Pellucid, PGA of America, ASGCA, Golf Course Superintendants Association of America [GCSAA], USGA, Golf 20/20, and the National Sporting Goods Association.)

GOLF *WAS* A SPORT

"Golf is a sport, not a game; and this distinction is fundamental if one is to attain a correct perspective of it, for both are endowed with principles of a different character."

—MAX BEHR

Old-time architect and accomplished amateur golfer Max Behr believed that golf should remain true to its origin as a "sport." The runner-up in the 1908 U.S. Amateur to Jerome Travers, Behr insisted that golf must not transform into a "game."

Alister MacKenzie made fun of his good friend for "quibbling" over words. However, Behr's point may help explain why modern golf seems out of sync.

Golf initially thrived on linksland, and the golfer had to deal with wind, gorse, and sandy pits. Like hunting or fishing, it was man versus what nature put before him. The golfer dealt with whatever disaster came his way.

"Golf was then in that fortunate state when it never entered the mind of the golfer that he could vie with nature," Behr wrote.

Games, on the other hand, pit at least two opponents of the human variety who square off over a prepared ground. The playing surface should do its best to not favor sides.

"A game is enclosed in principles, strictly speaking, because everything about it is man-made," Behr wrote. "He levels the ground according to a predetermined scheme, marks it off, and superimposes a logical idea upon it. He is in every way master of the situation and, to him, the surface of the earth is merely one of the exact tools of the pastime he creates."

Detailed rules are created to police games while allowing the battles to be played at a reasonable pace. The first two foul balls became strikes in baseball, for example. Tennis provides just two serving chances per point to land one in the service court.

Modern golf has been transformed into a *game*, replete with expectations for gamelike equity at all times. The rule book is longer than a Tom Clancy novel. And yet all of these rules will never completely eliminate the "rub of the green" and other assorted natural calamities left over from golf's sporting days.

To keep the game as "fair" as possible, golf courses are now supposed to minimize the opportunity for imperfect play and counteract advantages gained through new equipment by adding length, rough, trees, and softer conditions. Regardless of a course's character and architectural intent, rigging devices are brought in to control the play, theoretically rewarding the straight while punishing the wayward. Trees are planted to cut off escape routes. Bunkers are shifted or added to restrict the success of the megadriver that launches drives like a cannon.

In this effort to close openings, seal fates, and protect the "integrity" of the game, something insidious happened. Not only do these elements still fail to dish out punishment equitably, but also bunkers, golf's ultimate hazard, must now be immaculately raked so as to make the player's recovery shot fair!

"What is the cry we hear today—this or that is unfair!" Behr wrote in 1922. "A golfer comes in from a round, and some bunker or green has spoiled his score, and he proceeds to damn the course and the whole world. And all this because he approaches golf selfishly, with such an exaggeration of ego that he is convinced he is not only equal to coping with nature, but that he should never be humbled by her."

As course conditions have been refined and the golfer's equipment perfected, golf course designers and superintendents are asked to keep the game tough but "fair" for the combatants. Throw in sudden changes in technology and another bizarre ingredient is added to the mix.

It was the governing bodies' job to keep golf a sport by ensuring that equipment did not become as important as human skill. They failed, and

---

AND YOU THOUGHT THOSE WORDS WERE TOUGH . . .

Five years after first making his case for golf the sport versus
the game, Max Behr pointed out more consequences of constant distance increases caused by golf ball innovation and a
lack of governing-body interest in the long-term effects on shotmaking and golf architecture.

Here is what Behr had to say when he wrote "The Ball Problem" in *The Country Club Magazine* in 1927:

> What we are witnessing today is not any high degree of skill
> in stroking the ball, but the mere control of physical power in
> hitting it. The deterioration of skill brought about by the pres-
> ent ball has caused a mischievous repercussion throughout the
> length and breadth of golf. The inordinate distance the ball can
> now be driven has caused in golf architecture a very definite in-
> firmity of principle as all deductions from quantity values are apt
> to induce. Quantity must be opposed by quantity. Consequently
> the size of our greens and the width of our fairways have become

---

now the "game" is out of whack. With superlong drives and new course
records, we can expect more requests to trick up our "game boards."

Plant more trees. Pinch those landing areas. Install new tees. Do *something* to protect our slope rating and get to work to prevent those young
guns from embarrassing our home course with a 67. Oh, and can we rake
the bunkers *twice* a day?

"I do not mean to imply that it is possible to return to those halcyon
days of golf, or that it is even desirable," Behr wrote. "But what I do wish
to emphasize is that unless we keep before us a true perspective of golf,
a viewing of it always from its natural side, it will eventually degenerate
to a known quantity, a true game, and will become robbed of those elements of mystery and uncertainty which make every round a voyage of
discovery. The fate of golf would seem to lie in the hands of the Royal

restricted, and the rough made damnable. Instead of being an art where the medium penalty is used to create ideas calling for intelligent application of skill, golf architecture has become a system of penology. Thus instinct is met by instinct, and under the stimulus of impulse the mind is subject to the delusion that two wrongs can make a right. Little is being done to curb instinct; our fairways are mere troughs through which it is allowed to vent itself. We are locking up this wild desire for distance just as we cage wild animals.

And a further effect, especially noticeable in the United States, is the demand to keep the greens in a soft condition. The golfer cannot stop the ball so the greens must. This has caused over-watering which has seriously damaged the health of the turf. Indeed the evil ramifications caused by the present ball could fill a book.

The question before the golfers of the world is plain as a pike-staff. Are they going to be sportsmen and accept a ball that requires skill to propel, or, in their infantile worship of mere distance, are they going to continue to be downright game-hogs?

and Ancient Golf Club and the United States Golf Association. Can we expect that they will protect and reverence the spirit of golf?"

No, Mr. Behr, they have not.

PAINTING OVER OUR MASTERPIECES

"I think it's a tragedy that we are seeing all the golf courses change their layouts for golf. It's out of control. To me it's a tragedy."

—HAL SUTTON

Golf courses are living, breathing things. Yes, they evolve. Sometimes for the better, oftentimes in ways that would make their creators downright queasy.

A green chairman filled in at least thirty bunkers at Cypress Point just a few years after the course opened to worldwide acclaim in 1928. The green chairman in question was a dreadful golfer. He was also acting practically (in his mind anyway). The club was struggling to survive during the Depression, so voila, let's get rid of expensive bunkers that I find annoying.

Cypress Point has recently finished reinstalling all of those bunkers. Many other wonderful courses have undertaken similar restorations. After initial protests resisting change, members realize that their courses needed to be dusted off and rejuvenated to make their golf more enjoyable.

But now the word "restoration" is taking on a new, more sinister, meaning. No longer are courses reinstalling lost features or enlarging shrunken greens. Instead, they are aiming to restore the "iron the architect intended golfers to use to approach this green." Or they are doing bizarre things "in the spirit of (fill in architect's name here)."

These old reliable courses are having the life strangled out of them to accommodate one of three factors: longer driving distances (needed in large part to counteract unregulated technology), the vain notion of protecting par (despite obvious advances in course conditioning, instruction, and equipment), or plastic surgery at the hands of egotistical

---

NEW LOOK (7,600-YARD)
TORREY PINES: NOT AGING WELL

Though no one would have labeled Torrey Pines South a masterpiece, it was one of the better public courses in Southern California. In 2002 it was lengthened to 7,600 yards and "doctored" by Rees Jones to get it ready for a future U.S. Open. When it debuted at the 2003 Buick Invitational, Tour players gave positive assessments, not wanting to hurt the feelings of locals excited about their new $3 million product.

When the players returned to the course in 2004, the new-look Torrey Pines had recently been awarded the 2008 U.S. Open.

Tom Pernice Jr., after a 3-under 69 in the third round, said, "This is an old, traditional seaside course, but now it looks like it was built in 2003 and it is a typical piece of junk that Rees Jones designs. This was one of the great traditional courses until they changed it."

"It plays like it is 14,000 yards," said Dennis Paulson, who had played the course as a San Diego native and Golden State Tour graduate. "For some reason the USGA likes Rees Jones. I don't know why—if he's got dirty pictures of the USGA or what. I think he's absolutely clueless as a designer. He has no imagination, because he can't see past himself. He's got an ego bigger than anything you can imagine."

"I guess I'm a traditionalist," said Bob Tway, who won here in 1986. "I have played here since 1985. So when they changed it, I just don't like it at all. The greens are just totally different. There is no imagination to the greens as far as the lay of the land."

---

architects, who want to get their names in lights next to Tillinghast and Ross.

Some of the great works of art—the equivalent of Van Goghs and Monets—are going to be lost largely because of the USGA's inaction and

---

its suggestion to alter the courses to accommodate technology instead of confronting the disease that threatens their lives.

Sadly, the owners, caretakers, and architects entrusted to preserve the classics have joined in on the scheme. Some are retrofitting classic works of art by tacking on features that do not fit (usually because they don't know how to match the old architecture's subtlety). At the same time, they are adding more time, difficulty, and boredom to a sport that is already losing customers for those very reasons.

Would an art museum respond to complaints that their Renoir's and Rembrandt's are poorly lit by commissioning someone to repaint the canvases with brighter colors? Would the Louvre bring in Leroy Neiman to jazz up those dark Renaissance portraits so that visitors could make out the faces better? No, they'd fix the lighting and leave the masterpieces alone.

As C. B. Macdonald once wrote after seeing "novel" advances in course design, "the very soul of golf shrieks." Golf is painting over its masterpieces for the wrong reason. And all because "progress" has been embraced as golf's savior.

PART II

TECHNOLOGY:

*Failing to Make Golf More Fun,
More Affordable, or More Interesting*

"Technological progress has merely provided us with more efficient means for going backwards."

—ALDOUS HUXLEY

PGA Tour driving distances increased a foot per year from 1968 to 1995 thanks largely to subtle technological improvements, better athletes, the advent of practice, and better instruction. In the early twenty-first century, golf saw huge yearly distance increases thanks to the erosion of regulation that was designed to protect the integrity of the sport. Here's how it happened.

DEREGULATION

"What we call progress is the exchange of one nuisance for another nuisance."

—Havelock Ellis

Airplane manufacturers could make a commercial jetliner that flies faster, allowing passengers to get across the country in a couple of hours. But a faster jet would require longer runways. Most airports would have to undertake costly retrofits or face obsolescence because they lack the land to expand runways. New airports would have to be built to accommodate the progressive jet, which in major cities means a new facility an hour outside of town. These faster jets would also consume more fuel, meaning more cost for passengers on top of whatever added airport "service fees" were tacked on to fund the new airport construction.

In other words, nothing about a faster flying jet makes much economic sense for the airlines or the passengers. Who wants to drive an extra hour to save 2 hours in the air, with tickets costing twice as much?

It's a trade off no reasonable businessperson or customer would stand for, yet this type of nonsensical and unprecedented acceptance of deregulation is exactly what has happened in golf. The sport is trying to accommodate a version of the faster jet at consumer expense, in the form of longer flying golf balls.

Even though the USGA created a test to prevent this scenario, the ball manufacturers figured out ways to get around those tests; the USGA, afraid to admit complicity, cowered. Golf has been deregulated.

"Deregulation essentially boosts returns by throwing some people over the side—usually people in the bottom half get priced out—but during hard

economic patches those 'liberated' industries are always back at government's door, demanding assistance."

—WILLIAM GREIDER, *THE SOUL OF CAPITALISM* (2003)

At great expense, existing golf courses are expanding, and newly built designs have been getting longer for decades. In the early twentieth century, a respectable, "normal" eighteen-hole course went from 6,000 yards spread over 100 acres to 7,000 yards over at least 150 acres, more often close to 200.

Now, some courses are unable to keep up with the accelerating and changing dynamics of deregulated golf, where distance increases have gone from subtle to incredible. Some courses' lack of flexibility threatens their very existence.

It doesn't matter that some of these layouts have devoted 80 or 90 years of great service to golf and probably give most golfers plenty of trouble. They are seen as obsolete, so they try to remain relevant by growing rough and planting trees that needlessly tax the golfer, just so the course will be perceived as difficult and worthy of a "championship" label.

Even worse, once-safe playing corridors have become unsafe now that golfers can slice a ball onto adjoining holes thought to be out of reach when the course was created.

Meanwhile, new courses are being built to top the outdated ones, but few capture the character of the classics. When the new layouts are 7,200 yards long and built for a power game, the recreational golfer quickly grows tired of trying to play them. Or, at best, golfers play them less often than they would if the course had been a shorter, more playable design.

Regulation has been undermined because golf equipment companies believe the road to Fortune 500 heaven is traveled by marketing the newest, longest flying ball and the biggest, easiest-to-hit driver. So they outsmarted the USGA test and with a few threats, bullied their way around the rules. The USGA, armed with a test to take back control and fearful of being branded socialists for interfering with the "free market," shelved regulation.

The manufacturers deregulated the industry without having to go to court, pay a pricey lobbyist, or persuade anybody of anything except the great service they provide to golf. At least in the real world when politicians are bought and paid for, we can understand why such deregulation takes place. But the USGA hasn't been bought and paid for.

"Regulatory agencies that focused on a single sector were always vulnerable to capture by the regulated industry itself . . ."
—WILLIAM GREIDER, *THE SOUL OF CAPITALISM* (2003)

The USGA was caught off guard by technology and will have trouble catching up unless they decide to accept a backdoor solution such as the competition-ball concept, which allows them to save face (and will be explored later in this book).

The USGA has been outmaneuvered and out-marketed by the industry they hoped to regulate. And now golf stagnates. So, guess what? Certain companies want the USGA, the PGA Tour, and other nonprofit organizations to spend money to grow the game so those corporations can profit!

To the corporations' dismay, play is down in deregulated golf. There aren't enough consumers to meet projected future earnings. These liberated equipment companies have priced out the golfers with the combination of expensive equipment and a sport less fun or affordable to play. Hundreds of courses are now for sale because their overpriced, over-lengthened designs have run customers off to other pursuits.

How long will it be before equipment companies start coming to the governing bodies for financial bailouts when business is *really* bad?

Regulation was put in place because golf has to be more than just a distance and consumption chase. Shotmaking, creativity, imagination, and a diverse number of ways to get to the hole are becoming artifacts of the past. A one-dimensional sport that emphasizes power isolates average or below-average participants.

Golf has passed the added costs that come with deregulation to its dwindling customer base. Customers, faced with cheaper and less punishing nongolf alternatives, ultimately bail—or play less often than they'd like.

HOW THE USGA BLEW IT: SHELVING OPTIMIZATION

"Now, to keep pace with the increase in technological wizardry pumped out by ball manufacturers, the USGA has had to take its testing to a higher level. And Iron Byron, sad to say, just doesn't cut it anymore."

—*"A New Test Pattern," Golf Journal, May 1998*

Iron Byron was outsmarted. Hey, it happens. But the mechanical device that tested golf balls did its job for 20 years or so. Granted, the test was probably outdated when metal woods hit the market in the late 1980s. But don't forget, the USGA is alone when it comes to equipment testing. Their international counterpart, the Royal and Ancient Golf Club of St. Andrews (R&A), does no testing whatsoever and is, in general, completely useless on issues related to technology. In fact, the R&A rarely get the blame they deserve for dragging their feet on most issues, and the USGA has been kind in not pointing out the Royal and Ancient's ineptitude.

After announcing his retirement via a May 1998 *Golf Journal* cover story, Iron Byron is pulling a Michael Jordan. He's coming out of retirement. And boy, are the manufacturers delighted!

The machine first known as Iron Mike was patterned after a fine golfer's swing that looked a lot like Byron Nelson through impact. *Golf Journal* editor Bob Sommers later claimed credit for naming the machine Iron Byron.

Using a persimmon driver and striking the ball at 109 miles per hour, Iron Byron made contact at a fixed launch angle, sending drives out onto the USGA's big front lawn. It was a tough machine to adjust, so the launch angle stayed the same even though testers knew that say, a rock-like Top Flite, launched at a 19-degree angle, would easily exceed the USGA's Overall Distance Standard (ODS).

For a while the USGA put a Band-Aid on this flaw by creating the "one-ball condition," where players could only use one-brand-per-round so that a good golfer could not pull out a Top Flite on the par 5s and a softer Maxfli on par 3s.

That solved the problem until the mid-1990s when the companies started introducing balls with Top Flite's distance characteristics, only the covers felt and reacted like softer, balata-covered balls that had kept better players using softer, shorter flying balls. This meant that good players, who launch it differently from Joe Hack, were going to create conditions that caused the ball to exceed the USGA's limit, known as the Overall Distance Standard.

As testing director Frank Thomas worked with the Iron Byron test, he and his staff foresaw the likelihood that innovations in ball cover design and club fitting would lead to the predicament we are in today. Before he left the organization and became a consultant and a contributor to *Golf Digest*, Thomas led the creation of the Indoor Test Range (ITR) in the late '90s that addressed the problem of varying launch angles and inconsistent testing conditions. The new test would retire Iron Byron and actually made it possible to cap the maximum overall distance the ball flew, no matter who was at the wheel of the car and what engine was driving their ball.

Besides being called the Indoor Test Range, this test was also referred to as "optimization." It could predict how any ball would perform, regardless of ball-launch angle and speed. According to several USGA sources, the ball manufacturers witnessed the development of the optimization test, with many company officials seeing the test during visits to Far Hills, New Jersey.

Yet, in 1999 when plans to eventually shift testing to optimization were announced, the manufacturers claimed to be surprised. They also insisted the test did not accurately reflect how a golf ball would be struck and worse, expressed outrage that they didn't have any input on optimization (even though several prominent figures in the golf equipment industry were well aware of its scientific properties).

Why did manufacturers change their position? It became apparent that optimization would permanently cap potential technology-aided increases for the best players. And since the manufacturers rely on marketing the latest distance-boosting equipment, this test could not be allowed to become permanent.

The first news of the USGA's decision to abandon Iron Byron in favor of the ITR came in 1998 when the USGA and Callaway were locked in the "springlike effect" driver debate. (A standard for springlike effect has since been agreed upon after the Royal and Ancient finally decided to get on the same page as the USGA and set limits on spring effect.) This was also the time many golf companies had become publicly traded entities, raising the stakes and creating a cutthroat competitive attitude never before seen in the golf equipment business.

The indoor test was doomed in late 2000 when Frank Thomas left the USGA "to pursue other interests." Or, as Frank Hannigan wrote in *Golf Digest*, "organizational code for 'the two parties could no longer stand each other.'"

After Thomas's departure, no public explanation was ever given for dumping the optimization test in favor of bringing a new and improved Iron Byron back. One could assume that either the indoor test really didn't work very well, as the USGA now claims, or more likely it would have made many of the balls now on the market illegal and forced the USGA to make its case against technology, exposing itself to lawsuits and unpopularity with golfers.

Current USGA technical director Dick Rugge, a former Taylor Made club design and testing executive, insists that he, too, was skeptical of the manufacturers' reaction, but his own scientific view agreed that the optimization test was not "relevant to what best players were doing."

However, the decision to eliminate "optimization" looks even worse in light of the replacement test's (called Phase II) loopholes and the sudden 20-yard distance increases seen in 2003, created thanks to optimizing launch conditions.

Here's how the companies will continue to outsmart the USGA's new Phase II test, better known as the triumphant return of Iron Byron. The manufacturers can create balls that will pass the Iron Byron test under its fixed launch conditions. But these balls can conceivably exceed the overall distance maximum if launched a few degrees differently. With

THERE IS NO LIMIT TO SCIENCE

When the USGA came out with the specs for its new ball test in 2003, they announced, "Any additional distance gains will not be due to design or construction changes in the ball itself."

Former USGA testing director Frank Thomas says the ball has reached its maximum and that significant "near-term increases (3 to 4 yards) will only come from matching players launching conditions to approximate the optimum launching condition for a particular ball design, plus increases in club head speed."

So far Thomas's prediction has proven true. But those who insist that limits have been reached have been saying that for years, even though we've watched the most dramatic distance surges in golf history in just the last 2 years—after the USGA told us the situation was under control.

Those folks might want to remember the words of Alister MacKenzie, who prophesied about the ball and science way back in 1934:

> Today, many are trying to obtain a temporary advantage by buying the latest far-flying ball on the market. It is often suggested that we have already got to the limit of flight of a golf ball. I do not believe it, as there is no limit to science. During the war, experts told us we had got to the limit of flight of a cannonball, then the Germans invented a gun which propelled a shell three times as far as it had ever been sent before.

advanced fitting equipment that allows companies to match golfers with drivers that are best suited to their personal launch conditions, the club fitting monitors can determine an optimum angle and spin rate that even the soon-to-be-updated Iron Byron won't be able detect.

Optimization would have prevented this. Again, Rugge refutes that notion but at the same time, also makes clear that this test was designed

---

"THEY DISAPPEARED"

If you still are not convinced that the USGA has knowingly compromised the future of golf by allowing manufacturers to dictate standards or by supporting the myth that technology innovation is vital to growing the sport, consider these profound comments from the USGA's Dick Rugge. In a March 2001 interview for *Golf Journal*, Rugge had recently joined the USGA technical staff:

> Golf is meant to be a broad and deep challenge of a golfer, and we want to make sure equipment doesn't alter the balance it should have with skill in such a way that the challenges become less in the game.
>
> We have to do something before it happens rather than after it happens. Our mission is to protect the game. In 1975, the high-water mark of tennis participation in the U.S. reached about 34 million players. About the same time, the oversize racket was brought to the U.S. to make the game more enjoyable and easier

around equipment on the marketplace. Though Rugge makes his points eloquently, the idea that the USGA is working around the marketplace pains many former USGA presidents and staffers who see a regulatory body fearful of regulation. The situation is made even more painful when USGA rules are completely optional for golfers and companies to play by.

The new and improved Byron has moved indoors and swings faster (120 mph). He finally uses a driver made out of something other than wood (a titanium head with a steel shaft that has an .820 Coefficient of Restitution [COR] instead of the .790 COR for laminated wood), and Byron's launch angle condition is similar to Tiger Woods's (10 degrees and 2,520 RPM, respectively). A big alarm goes off if he hits the ball over 320 yards.

---

to play and more fun and all those kind of things. From 1975 to 1985, one decade later, the elite game of tennis had markedly changed. It became a power game. The finesse that had been present before was largely gone, and it wasn't so interesting to people anymore. And that 34 million had shrunk to about 13 million—interestingly enough, about the same ratio as bowling. And according to people at the United States Tennis Association, the hard-core tennis players stayed. The ones lost were the marginal players, the ones the game was trying to turn into hard-core players. They disappeared.

Now I can't say for sure it was the oversize tennis racket that drove them all away, but it sure didn't keep them in the game. I think it's our responsibility not to allow unchecked technology experiments, like they had in bowling and tennis, to come into golf. To be true to our mission of protection, we can't take these kinds of chances, especially when other sports have shown that an easier game resulting from equipment 'advances' is not the road to more participation.

More importantly, since the USGA announced the updated Phase II procedure, no company has threatened to file a lawsuit. Why? Because they aren't worried.

The vice president of club and ball research at Taylor Made (owner of the Maxfli brand), told *Golf World* during the summer of 2003, "There's still some room for the balls being played on tour to get a little faster under this proposal."

So the test can still be outsmarted. More importantly, as Rugge was quick to point out during the Phase II unveiling, no ball currently on the market would be found illegal.

Why does the new Phase II test "work around" balls that might have been illegal under previous tests? And why is the USGA going to use a testing device that will continue to be outsmarted?

Perhaps because the USGA believes manufacturers have successfully demonized the governing body in the eyes of most golfers, criticizing it for withholding progressive equipment from the consumer's hands, and thus, harming golf's chance to grow. Characterizing the USGA as a roadblock to free market happiness is clearly a shrewd way to go because the USGA rarely fights back in the press. And some golfers were understandably still hostile toward the USGA when it seemed possible that expensive and already approved drivers might be declared illegal in 1998.

But a $500 golf club is different than a $3 golf ball.

New golf balls that comply with golf's version of a common-sense cap could be quickly reintroduced into golf, with the "hot" balls becoming collector's items (or sold to noncompetitive golfers who have no interest in playing by the *optional* USGA rules). But the USGA has mysteriously gone out of its way to make it clear that no balls currently on the market will be deemed nonconforming—as if golf balls are difficult and costly to replace in a short time.

Most of all, the manufacturers still seem to have the USGA right where they want it: running scared.

THE STATE OF THE GAME

THE GOLF CHANNEL HOSTS A ROUND-TABLE DISCUSSION IN 2003

Not since David Fay and Ely Callaway faced off in a live debate had the Golf Channel aired such a significant issue-oriented show.

The 90-minute "State of the Game" was hosted by Golf Channel business reporter Adam Barr in December 2003 to discuss how golf was on the verge of a breakthrough (according to a four-page *New York Times* special advertising spread).

The lively panel started off with a President's Cup debate and several remarked how great things are in golf. Awareness is up, growth exists, the sport has never been healthier.

But under the glare of those notoriously hot studio lights, the panel eventually started to paint a less-than-rosy picture. Greg Hopkins, CEO of equipment manufacturer Cleveland Golf, was the first to speak up. "We're setting ourselves up for a fall down the road," he said. "And if we're patting ourselves on the back and saying it is healthy, I think we're building a house with termites."

Much of the "State of the Game" focused on whether the golf ball is going too far and harming the sport. Opinions varied as to the cause of the sudden distance surges since 2000, though oddly, most of the conversation often turned to scoring, as opposed to the quality of golf played or the effect rapid distance increases have on architecture.

At least the show provided theories about why we have seen huge distance surges in the new century.

"What the ball guys have done is take a two-piece ball within the same rules the USGA has had and they figured out how to soften it up and make it spin," said Hopkins.

"The biggest reason for distance increases in the last two or three years, not the last ten, starts with the Tour player finding out how to maximize launch conditions," said Taylor Made CEO Mark King, reinforcing that the USGA's "Iron Byron" test was outsmarted by the manufacturers and that the "optimization" test would have prevented such a change.

"Once we found that out, I can tell you that's what's making these 20-yard differences. Higher launch, less spin, speed is the same, the ball goes 20 yards farther," King continued. "You're not going to stop that. That isn't the face [of the club], that isn't the length of the shaft. That isn't how strong the guy is. That's a launch condition that optimizes the distance and that's the biggest single [difference]. We've got hundreds of tour players that come in every single week and all they work on are maximizing their launch conditions. And when they find the right one they put on 10–15 yards."

Jack Nicklaus continued his campaign for a "competition ball" and pointed out that on the tour today, "80 percent of the game is power."

Mark King also agreed that golf is now a power game, though it was difficult for viewers to tell if he thought this was a good or bad thing. "All the tournaments today are won by the longest players. Vijay Singh is long, Ernie is long, Tiger is long. You have no short players today that have any chance to be a consistent winner."

Ladies Professional Golf Association (LPGA) tour commissioner Ty Votaw insisted that golf's popularity is tied to power. "What fascinates the public with respect to any sport?" Votaw asked. "When you tune into 'SportsCenter,' do they show a pick and roll in basketball? No, they show the slam dunk. Do they show hit and run in baseball? No, they show the home run. The highlights and power game fascinate the public in every sport and I think we have to have a mind-set to understand what brings people into the game is a fascination with things like power."

Actually, ESPN's "SportsCenter" and the Golf Channel's "Golf Central" show highlights of chip-ins, precise approach play, great recovery shots, successful long putts, and every once in a while, a player driving a short par 4. They do not show the day's longest drives.

Regardless of whether distance is caused by optimized launch conditions or better athletes, the panel said golf was more popular than ever

---

THEY'RE BETTER ATHLETES!

At the 2004 USGA winter meeting, vice president Walter Driver insisted that "75 percent" of the distance increase on the PGA Tour can be attributed to "player athleticism."

The athleticism excuse took a hit in 2004 when long-driving but "stocky" athletes such as Craig Parry, John Daly, Joey Sindelar, Craig Stadler, and Meg Mallon all drove the ball a country mile en route to winning important tournaments in 2004.

At age 58, Champions Tour player Gil Morgan averaged 291 yards off the tee in 2004—30 yards longer than his Tour driving distance average in 1984. Morgan was asked why he and all other seniors are so much longer today.

"I think more of the players are working out in the off-season," Morgan said.

Meanwhile, the svelte Stadler drives it 23 yards longer in 2004 than he did in his prime 20 years ago. And in 2004, Tom Purtzer, once the longest driver on the Tour who has undergone three hip surgeries and endures ongoing back pain, still managed to drive the ball 26 yards longer on average than he did in 1994.

---

thanks to the technology-fueled power game. Opinions varied on whether this was translating to more rounds played.

Mark King said play was up even though it's been widely reported that play is way down. "I think people are coming in [to the sport], they're playing and they're enjoying it and the facilities are getting better, and there's more facilities. I think it's getting less expensive to play golf and I think if you really get to the facts of the game, this is a great game and it's in great shape."

Getting less expensive to play golf? Maybe in Myrtle Beach where nearly half the courses are on the verge of bankruptcy and green fees have been cut out of desperation.

David Pillsbury, former CEO of American Golf who led the company during its final days before it was snapped up by Goldman Sachs to

---

fend off bankruptcy, offered a different view of the golf-course industry. "There's momentum around more outreach to fill the golf courses up, which, frankly, are hurting. A lot of golf course's rounds are down, in many cases 10,000 rounds."

Frank Thomas, former testing director for the USGA, pointed out that "commercialization is actually starting to stifle the game. I think the cost to players is creating a problem."

Though the connection between longer courses and more expensive golf for everyday players was never discussed, many on the panel agreed that it's easier to change golf courses than testing rules or golf balls. Of course, there were no golf-course owners present to refute this notion.

"Let's get the golf courses narrowed up to be able to defend themselves," said John Cook, who sees tighter fairways as a way to mute longer driving distances, to return strategy, and to reintroduce shotmaking.

Cleveland Golf's CEO Greg Hopkins took it a step further.

"Golf's got an advantage though," said Hopkins. "Because you can add a new bunker. You have a dynamic playing field that can address change in the game. You may not like it, but you can address it."

To which Jack Nicklaus asked, "Who is going to pay for it? Who pays for it?"

WAIT, SO THE EQUIPMENT DOESN'T MATTER?

EQUIPMENT-MANUFACTURER SPIN GONE AWRY

"Corporation, n. *An ingenious device for obtaining individual profit without individual responsibility."* —AMBROSE BIERCE

Sometimes surprises come in all shapes and sizes. None was more special than this gem cooked up by the marketing folks at Titleist who emailed their press release to Golf Writer's Association of America members the morning after the tedious 2003 U.S. Open.

Apparently the folks down at Titleist spent their weekend preparing to spin the 2003 U.S. Open after several eye-opening 400-yard drives rendered an already dull course even less interesting to watch. Players slugged their way around until one emerged as the golfer who messed up the least.

Thrilling stuff!

If this is the future of golf, many of us are going to be watching something else. Yet the people at Titleist excitedly announced the arrival of the Power Game. To hear them tell it, the 350–400 yard drives we saw at the 2003 U.S. Open were *not* sending professional golf to "the edge of ruin." Furthermore, the Power Game wasn't helping the players score better, according to Titleist.

If this assertion is the case—that everything is rosy and the best players are *not* helped by technology—then why should anyone buy the latest Titleist equipment? If scores were not better because of the Power Game, why embrace the new balls and drivers that Titleist says are *not* improving scoring?

From Wally Uihlein, CEO of Acushnet (Titleist):

POWER GAME DOES NOT GUARANTEE
SUCCESS AT U.S. OPEN

Fairhaven, MA (June 16, 2003)

To anybody who witnessed or watched the 103rd U.S. Open at Olympia Fields, the arrival of the Power Game and the distances achieved by some players are not bringing professional golf to the edge of ruin as recently expressed by a vocal minority. If professional golf is experiencing some irreparable harm, it was certainly not identified at the U.S. Open.

[Author's interruption: The arrival of the Power Game was such a thrilling moment that the 2003 U.S. Open final-round television ratings were down 44 percent from the previous year's last day.]

Are players hitting the golf ball longer? No doubt. The average driving distance at the U.S. Open for all rounds was 288 yards. Was it reflected in the overall scoring? Not by a long shot. The scoring average of all 155 players in the field was 72.38, more than 2-over par. Some additional facts:

The average driving distance for the final round was 295.8 yards, yet the average score was 73 or 3-over par.

A total of 20 players averaged more than 300 yards in driving distance for the week, only four of whom finished among the top 10 in scoring. *[Author's note: The winner, Jim Furyk, was not using Titleist equipment.]*

Sixty-eight players made the cut, which came at 3-over-par 143, and is the lowest cut ever at the U.S. Open in terms of score and the second lowest in relation to par. However, only 27 players finished the tournament at 3-over par or better.

[Author's note: So let's get this straight: The Power Game arrived and weekday scores broke records. The weekend scores were high because of the Power Game's decision to take the weekend off after helping set records? Which is it?]

11 of the 20 players who averaged more than 300 yards in driving distance finished between 33rd and 66th in scoring. The top two players in driving distance finished 57th (+10) and 42nd (+6), respectively, in scoring.

The U.S. Open champion placed 25th in driving distance with an average of 295 yards. He also was 2nd in driving accuracy (70%), and was 1st in greens in regulation (74%).

The winning score of 272 tied a record for the lowest 72-hole score in U.S. Open history, also achieved in 2000 (Pebble Beach), 1993 (Baltusrol) and 1980 (Baltusrol).

While there were 24 players under par after the first round and 26 players under par through 36 holes of play, only four players finished with sub-par totals for the tournament. Only one player has finished under par in the first two major championship tournaments of the 2003 season.

Over the course of 24 PGA Tour events this year through the U.S. Open Championship, three players in their 20s have combined for five wins, with the youngest winner being age 27; and four player[s] in their 40s have combined for five wins, with the oldest being age 47. *[Author's note: And the point of all this is? High scores and old guys mean technology isn't helping? Or is it helping?]*

While confronted by changes with players' physical fitness and strength, course conditions, and equipment technology, the professional game continues to grow and prosper because the rules in place more than adequately control technological influence. *[Author's note: The rules in place were so good, that the Tour subsequently had to step in and institute a driver test for 2004 while threatening the USGA to get its act together on ball testing. And the game grows and prospers so much that the commissioner is spending most of his time begging sponsors to stay on board, while rounds played plummet.]*

As evidenced by the performances at the U.S. Open and at PGA Tour events throughout the year, players' abilities should enjoy upper case recognition. After all, as the tagline says, "these guys are good!" *[Author's note: End of press release.]*

Their ads suggest that Titleist equipment makes the game easier and more fun because their technologically superior stuff allows golfers to hit the ball longer and straighter, and thus, leads to better scoring. And who doesn't admire the consistency of Titleist equipment? It's beautifully made and has always been a name golfers associate with quality.

But according to their very *own* press release, even though Titleist equipment allowed certain players to drive the ball unprecedented distances, it didn't help them score any better.

So if the Pro V-1, Titleist wedges, putters, and assorted Titleist drivers didn't help Ernie, Phil, and Vijay score, how could it help Joe Average? Why pay all that money for something the company admits does not help its best players?

The Power Game certainly didn't make golf more interesting to watch, so why not regulate distance to return exciting shotmaking and decision-making scenarios that the average golfer can relate to?

BLAME THE MEDIA!

In a July 2003 issue of *Sports Illustrated*'s "Golf Plus" supplement, Wally Uihlein, Acushnet CEO, wrote a short commentary to refute the famous magazine's coverage of technology, and in particular, to complain about comments from noted teaching professional Mitchell Spearman. Spearman wrote that on the PGA Tour on "any given week, up to a quarter of the field could have illegal drivers, and I believe that some players use hot balls."

Uihlein, eager not to see any kind of cap put on the golf ball for fear of losing what Titleist perceives to be its only marketing opportunity, wrote, "The issue here is not Mr. Spearman's credibility on this subject, because clearly he has none. He is not a member of the PGA Tour, he is not a manufacturer, and he has not tested the equipment of every Tour member. The issue is why a leading publication like *Sports Illustrated* would provide a forum for slanderous allegations with no supporting evidence."

Having condemned one of the world's most respected teaching pros (talk about slander!) while criticizing a magazine that has established balanced coverage of golf issues, Uihlein went on to claim that "print and electronic media have promoted a technophobic agenda" and that this misleading coverage could lead to the PGA Tour adopting an "ill-conceived policy" dealing with technology.

"In its position paper on equipment," Uihlein wrote, "the PGA

When golfers feel pressured to buy the latest clubs and balls to attain longer driving distances to handle longer courses, that's going to be enough added cost to make some of them take up bird-watching or croquet (see the *New York Times*, May 23, 2003, article "Golf Starts Losing Grip and Croquet Moves In" if you don't believe me).

The Titleist message is actually quite clear: Technology is not ruining the sport. It is also not helping the best players in the world score

Tour says that the 'increased distance by today's elite players has proven to be problematical.' Among the reasons cited is 'an increasing media and fan perception that excellent play by today's professionals is more a result of technology than skill or athleticism.' Elsewhere in the document it says that 'to the extent golf-ball distance continues to increase and/or the perception of the media and the public relative to distance becomes more negative . . . the PGA Tour should further consider whether additional rule modifications are desirable.'"

Uihlein, who posed for the guest column with a photo of Bernard Goldberg's book on media *Bias*, then blamed the golf press for potentially ruining every consumer's opportunity to interact with future Titleist marketing campaigns tied to their favorite PGA Tour stars.

"Media and fan perceptions are unlikely to change as long as golf's Fourth Estate continues to distort the news and default on its obligation to be objective. If the Tour is serious about monitoring fan perception and using the feedback to affect policy going forward, then it needs to hold the media to a higher standard of balance than what is being practiced today."

Mind you, we are talking about media that rarely cover the technology subject, particularly the USGA's failure to institute its more advanced test. Meanwhile, the PGA Tour has skirted the issue for several years, hoping it would go away. Imagine how Uihlein will react when the tour does step in to protect its "product" and what will he say when the media cover that story?

better. However, buying the same Titleist equipment will help you, Average Golfer, score better.

This is what some people might call talking out of both sides of your mouth.

WHAT THE OLD GUYS SAID

(ABOUT THE BALL)

Innovation has been debated in golf since the late nineteenth century. From the featherie to the gutta to the Haskell, there were issues with size, weight, and cover design that had everyone weary of the issue by the late 1920s. Many of the great writers and architects insisted that the distance debate needed to be settled so that courses would not keep adjusting to new, longer-flying balls. Imagine what they'd say today: Golf looks like a dog chasing its tail, scaring off players and raising costs for those who stay around, all to sustain the equipment marketplace?

Well, here's what they said at various times between 1920 and 1936, before we had another World War, Jack, Tiger, and the Pro V1.

Bernard Darwin, writer: "The architects have done nobly; they have fought the good fight, but it ought not to be a fight. The fact that it threatens to become so is the fault of the ball. Whether or not the ball can ever be brought back to its proper limits is another story, but unless it can, the architects will be forever fighting an uphill battle."

Alister MacKenzie, architect of Augusta National: "Something very drastic ought to have been done years and years ago. Golf courses are becoming too long."

Henry Longhurst, writer: "The cricketeer agreed that it seemed preposterous to alter 36,000 golf holes to accommodate an unsanctioned change in one ball, and that if the makers of cricket balls suddenly produced one which a schoolboy could hit over the Lord's pavilion, the authorities would not increase the size of Lord's, but inform the ball-maker what he could do with his new ball."

William Flynn, architect of Shinnecock Hills: "All architects will be a lot more comfortable when the powers that be in golf finally solve the

---

LIKE CUTTLEFISH SQUIRTING OUT INK

"When there is a gap between one's real and one's declared aims, one turns as it were instinctively to long words and exhausted idioms, like a cuttlefish squirting out ink."

—GEORGE ORWELL

Not content to have a cowering USGA and R&A, CEOs from golf equipment manufacturers continued to claim in 2004 that the governing bodies were killing the game by restricting the marketplace.

"The rule-making bodies simply and as a matter of fact don't care about the business of golf," Callaway's now former CEO Ron Drapeau said at a January 2004 PGA show gathering to discuss the state of the game. "If the USGA and the R&A continue to take the position that there is only one game of golf and the equipment rules are set for the pros and the rest of us have to find a way to survive, I think we're in trouble.

"Reduce the distance the pros are hitting the ball, both with the driver and the 9-iron and all other clubs in the bag," Drapeau added. "The facts are, the majority of the gain in distance that has come at the professional level has come from improvements in the golf ball, plain and simple."

His comments would seem more heartwarming to those in favor of a "competition ball" or some form of regulation if Drapeau's motive was pure. More likely, the comments are aimed at breaking Titleist's domination of the ball market.

Speaking of Titleist, their CEO, Uihlein, cooked up this gem of gibberish to justify his position:

> The S-Curve of invention application imparts that little manifest progress will be seen at the front end (The Breakthrough Phase) as the user community (golf equipment manufacturers, players) attempts to refine the invention (first-generation large-

Continued on next page

---

headed titanium drivers and multiconstruction solid golf balls) for maximum benefit and gain.

Shortly thereafter, as the user community determines how to optimize the distinctive benefits of the inventions (The Exponential Phase), a significant acceleration in incremental performance occurs for a finite period of time. Finally, as the limits of technology are reached and the maximums of regulatory compliance are approached, the S-Curve enters its third and final phase (The Mature Phase) where the improvement is limited and gradual.

In 2003, the PGA Tour experienced the Exponential Phase of the S-Curve involving the invention and adoption of large-headed titanium drivers and multicomponent solid-construction golf balls.

In 2004, results from the recently completed West Coast Swing further validate the S-Curve premise and indicate that we have entered the Mature Phase where, regardless of effort, improvements and increases will be gradual and modestly incremental.

Uihlein remains opposed to a competition ball or minor distance rollback for the overall good of the game, even though he claims technology has reached the limit of providing big distance gains.

If the limit has been reached, how could a small rollback hurt?

ball problem. A great deal of experimentation is now going on and it is to be hoped that before long a solution will be found to control the distance of the elusive pill. If, as in the past, the distance to be gotten with the ball continues to increase, it will be necessary to go to 7,500- and even 8,000-yard courses and more yards mean more acres to buy, more course to construct, more fairway to maintain, and more money for the golfer to fork out."

A. W. Tillinghast, player, writer, architect: ". . . the fetish of distance is worshipped entirely too often and there should be a quick end to it."

THEY SAID IT, NOT I

Here's what golf's higher-ups have been saying about distance increases and the consequences for golf. Some believe "it's all good," as the kids are being raised to say so that they don't become discerning consumers. Notice that the "it's all good" crowd is profiting from the distance race (big shocker) or covering its rear end. Others, whose only interest is the health and character of the sport, aren't so positive.

Bill Campbell, former USGA president and captain of the R&A: "In a nutshell, the phenomenon of this eye-catching, longer-hitting trend—caused by new balls and clubs as well as stronger players, all-out swing instruction, and modern agronomy—is more easily corrected by just shortening the ball, i.e., putting a governor on it. Though politically challenging, this cure isn't rocket science or U.N. diplomacy. The issue cries out for concerted attention, resolve, and action—all with a sense of urgency."

Greg Norman: "Go to every manufacturer—I represent Titleist—and give them specifications of the ball that was required at Augusta National just for the Masters tournament. You say, OK, every manufacturer makes that ball. If I was a manufacturer, I would love it because I would sell more golf balls. Because amateurs would love to buy a golf ball that Tiger Woods played with the same specifications. So he's going to buy the one that did go longer and then the Augusta golf ball. I think there's a lot of merit to it, and I would support it."

David Fay, USGA executive director: "Today's golf courses are playing shorter for the best players than ever before. Whether this is a 'problem' or a natural evolution of a healthy sport depends on your point of view—and quite often, your age."

DISTANCE: IT'S ALL RELATIVE

"Pleasure in obtaining length is only a matter of relativity."

—ALISTER MACKENZIE

Distance is all relative. The recent advances in equipment definitely help the elite player most. But, let's assume the new clubs and balls are changing the average daily game of golf, and possibly not for the worse. Clubs are better made, easier on our bodies, and longer lasting.

Do these sudden increases in distance really make golf more fun or better?

If Jerry buys the new Z ball and Larry sees Jerry drive it 10 yards longer, Larry will buy the Z ball and reap the same benefits. That's great for the equipment companies, but over the last 5 years (and the next 50 years), how does this distance pursuit benefit golf or keep Jerry and Larry and their sons and daughters playing golf?

Rich Beem, athlete: "I think any limitation on golf balls is a terrible idea. We're hitting the ball farther because we're better athletes. It's not just the equipment. If we limit ourselves, we'll regress."

Frank Hannigan, former USGA executive director: "More distance results from changes made to drivers and, more recently, to balls that are designed to react with clubs by departing at a higher launch angle, and with less spin. Ironically, the technological changes do nothing for the average golfer; to take full advantage of equipment innovations, a player must be exceptionally consistent—close to a scratch player. When the average golfer hits a ball in the center of a club, it's an accident. . . . [Increased distance] leads to greater expense, to slower golf, and robs us of the meditative pleasure of comparison."

Tom Fazio, architect: "I think it's been exciting for golf. I think the public coming out here and watching those players on that practice tee and hitting those golf balls 280, 300 yards in the air, I think it's great for golf."

Jack Vickers, founder of The International tour event and Castle Pines Golf Course: "The lively golf ball is killing the game of golf. We're going to ruin this game if we don't do something. We need to make the game competitive again. The other day I saw a golfer hit a 5-iron 278 yards to a green. How crazy are we getting? It's going to be a pitch-and-putt game, and it won't be golf as we once knew it. The USGA has not taken the steps it should have taken. They've let this thing go way beyond where it should have gone."

Gary Player: "I can tell you right now this ball thing is coming to an end. Otherwise it'll be the demise of golf courses. . . . I guarantee as sure as I'm sitting here, the USGA has not had the leadership to do it, and I'm an admirer of the USGA. Something's going to be done in the future, but by whom, I'm not sure."

Nick Price: "Jack Nicklaus said it perfectly in an interview the other day. He said when he was in his prime, length was about 20 percent of the game. Now it's 80 percent. When you've got a great player like Jack Nicklaus, the greatest player of all time, saying that to people, why isn't someone listening?"

PART III

MAJOR IDENTITY CRISIS:

*How Professional Golf Has
Set a Dreadful Example in Its
Reaction to Deregulation*

"Ever since Woods won his first major, the '97 Masters by 12 shots, the American golf authorities, those he-men at Augusta National, the U.S. Golf Association and the PGA of America, have been trying to figure out ways to make courses Tiger-proof. This year their plans all came together: Make every major sheer drudgery, like the U.S. Open."

—MICHAEL BAMBERGER, IN HIS 2003 SPORTS ILLUSTRATED

POST-PGA CHAMPIONSHIP WRITE-UP

The Masters, U.S. Open, British Open, and PGA Championship are vital to the health of golf. The majors have inspired millions to take up golf because they attract enormous attention and television exposure.

The drama and thrills from events like Nicklaus's 1986 Masters win, Tiger's epic 2000 PGA playoff against Bob May, and Mickelson's 2004 Masters triumph over Ernie Els, have kept many frustrated golfers addicted to the sport while recruiting new blood. Such excitement also attracts a huge following of non-golfers. These are all good things.

The majors also influence maintenance of everyday courses and impact architectural trends. But as technology and stronger players have made many designs obsolete for the better player, the governing bodies and major associations like the PGA Tour attempt to keep pace with ever-longer distances. And as they declare that pro golfers have never been better athletes, the governing bodies cling to par as the standard, even though it's clearly outdated. This clash of ideals has impacted the character of golf's major championships with their goofy course setup ploys seeping into the everyday sport.

In the effort to stop Tiger and lower scores, they've all too often flattened the potential for excitement and fun that the majors should produce. Sadly, everyday golf often mimics the narrow fairway, high-rough, tree-lined fairway approach, which adds little to the recreational golfer's enjoyment of the sport.

Also discussed under the "Major Identity Crisis" banner is the death of the bunker in professional golf, the PGA Tour's failure to take advantage of the Tournament Players Club (TPC) concept as a way to generate exciting golf, and the possibility that the Tour might create its own set of rules to restore shotmaking.

OUT OF SYNC: THE GRAND SLAM

(AND WHY IT SETS A BAD EXAMPLE FOR ALL OF GOLF)

Two-time Masters champion Ben Crenshaw is "not ready" to agree that Grand Slam setups are too similar, "but an argument could be made that the four majors are now a lot more alike," he concedes. Crenshaw does, however, bemoan the similar approach to most modern-day championships.

"The players are dictated to as to how to play them. It's a defense mechanism in trying to govern a target score. And it's a reaction to what the equipment is doing. It's gotten us into this mess, into a morass of sameness."

Grand Slam golfing examinations used to go something like this: A player's long, preferably drawing tee shot and deft putting touch were rewarded at Augusta National. Controlled iron play didn't hurt either. Aggressive, even swashbuckling golf was encouraged at certain times, especially during Sunday's unpredictable final nine.

For the U.S. Open, every year in mid-June, players needed a completely different approach: centerline tee shots, ultraconservative course management, and plenty of patience. Swashbucklers need not make weekend hotel room reservations.

By July, low-flying wind shots, turtlenecks, and shotmaking creativity would be called upon at the charmingly unpredictable and brown-hued British Open. Players could swing a bit more aggressively. Then, just a few weeks later, the world's best players had to undo the kinks induced by linksland golf and recapture a target-style approach best suitable for a lush, inland PGA Championship layout.

The four majors still ask players to make seasonal adjustments, but time-tested course setups have been tinkered with in the Tiger Woods era, particularly at the Masters and the British Open. The seasons are becoming much less distinguishable.

At the Masters, former USGA President Will Nicholson oversaw the narrowing of Augusta National's trademark wall-to-wall fairways. In 1999 when the "second cut" was introduced, Nicholson actually stated that Masters's landing areas averaged "36.57 yards" in width.

Augusta's recent "premium on accuracy" mantra has translated to a premium on straightness off the tee. That's a bold departure from Jones's explicitly articulated desire to reward aggressive tee shot placement by allowing use of all portions of the wide fairways, depending on conditions, the day's hole location, and the player's preference.

But more troublesome in the Grand Slam scheme of things, Augusta's new setup philosophy is moving closer to the traditional arrangement found at the U.S. Open. Even at the thrilling 2004 Masters won by Phil Mickelson, the first three rounds consisted of dreadful plodding golf, transformed nearly overnight thanks to a brilliant final day setup that encouraged aggressive iron play.

One could argue that the U.S. Open has remained most faithful to its unique Grand Slam character. Narrow fairways, firm greens, and thick rough still reward patience and plodding as they have since Max Behr questioned playing through "hay fields" at Scioto in 1926. The USGA moved into the modern era by sometimes incorporating tightly mown chipping areas to reward creativity around certain greens. Players also have seen slightly shorter roughs that often entice them into unwise recovery attempts.

To offset these more democratic touches and the overall improvement in scoring ability, the USGA upped the ante on par protection in other ways. A couple of greens were too fast for their slopes at Southern Hills. A ridiculous hole location at Olympic Club and senseless fairway contouring at Bethpage revealed the USGA's struggle to balance its traditional identity with a modern game where better scores are inevitable. And they culminated this run of setup gaffes with the epic disaster at Shinnecock Hills (detailed later in this section).

NICK PRICE ON AUGUSTA AND LENGTH

In a November 2003 *Golf Digest* interview with Mike Stachura, Nick Price made several interesting comments about the new-look Augusta.

"I think the people at Augusta went the wrong way. They've made it a long hitters' course. People say, 'Well, Mike Weir's not a long hitter.' He's not short, trust me."

Price was then asked if Augusta was just "trying to keep the challenge the same in the face of technology."

"Well, I asked Byron Nelson about what they'd done with Augusta," Price replied. "And Byron, in his usual diplomatic way, said that he agreed with some of the things, but on the other points he wasn't so sure. And Phil Mickelson said something along the lines of, 'Well, I love the way they set up the majors now. If you look at the major championships, you've got Augusta, where you've got to hit the ball a long way, high, and you have to putt great. In the U.S. Open you've got to be straight,

The USGA will continue to struggle with setups until they accept the fact that a few more players reaching red figures will not undermine the stature or character of the U.S. Open.

Across the Atlantic, British Open links irrigate fairways that used to only rely on rain for moisture. They've also fertilized roughs for consistency and narrowed landing areas to widths that might even make a USGA committee squirm. Carnoustie's extreme setup showed that imposing a U.S. Open arrangement on a windy links will lead to goofy golf.

At recent opens—Royal Lytham, Muirfield, St. George's, and Troon—players left their drivers in the bag. A number of officials and players pointed to the higher winning scores as a barometer of success, a once unimaginable gauge of the Open championship's quality.

Americanized British Open venues look nothing like the crunchy, unpredictable links that used to provide a refreshing contrast to the year's

you don't have to be so long; you've got to keep your ball in the fairway, and you've got to chip and putt well. And the British Open is a shotmaker's paradise. You've got to manipulate the ball, hit it low, high and whatever. And the PGA's kind of a little bit of everything.'

"So I said to him, 'Do you mean to tell me that if you hit the ball 275 yards, now you can't win at Augusta? That's the first time in the history of the game that length has been a determining factor to whether you become a great player.'"

Price was then asked if golf was in danger of young players taking steroids to keep up with the times.

"If we put such an emphasis on length in the game, who knows? Every athlete is looking for an edge. If there's a kid, let's say, five-eleven, five-ten, great iron player, short on yardage, can't play on the team because there are four kids who hit it 320, how is he going to get on that team? That's when I think we'll be in trouble in a sport that's been basically drug free."

first two dipped-in-dark-green majors. The ensuing opens have not exactly recalled the glory years when players battled passionately over uneven pastures, oblivious to mottled aesthetics in their quest for golf's oldest title.

Meanwhile, the PGA Championship boosted its Grand Slam stock by balancing difficulty with enough room for players to maneuver. Engineered by senior director of tournaments Kerry Haigh, recent PGA Championship setups have encouraged players to use their drivers even in the face of extreme driving distances.

There were exceptions. The 1996 disaster of erecting a corporate tent on Valhalla's alternate seventh-hole fairway will go down in history as one of the great blunders.

Since learning that lesson, PGA setups started to compliment the host site's architecture while leaving a few openings to reward well-timed aggressiveness. The earth remained on its axis despite tournament leaders reaching double-digit, under-par figures. Epic finishes at Winged Foot, Medinah, Valhalla, Atlanta Athletic, Hazeltine, and Whistling Straits will be remembered as classic majors despite the red numbers.

Oak Hill briefly reversed the trend in 2003, with its stifling setup producing the Herculean Shaun Micheel–Chad Campbell back-nine showdown. The PGA of America and superintendent Paul Latshaw Jr. admitted that the rough had become more vicious than planned due to unexpected rains that ignited fertilizer that had been applied after a dry spring. Oak Hill was set up like a bad U.S. Open course and the result was ugly.

"If you drove into the Oak Hill rough, you chopped your ball out and made bogey," wrote Michael Bamberger in *Sports Illustrated*. "If you hit into the snarling half-foot rough around any of the greens, you took out your sand wedge, plopped the ball on, and made bogey. Oak Hill was an equal-opportunity golf course last week. Artistry took a beating."

Besides reducing the quality of golf and viewer interest, the modern-day major championship setup has muted the need for seasoning and experience that was once required to capture a major, making fluke winners more common in recent times. It used to take years for a golfer to acquire the imagination, intelligence, experience, creativity, inner calm, and flare for heroics that are hallmarks of a champion and a player who has paid his dues.

Capturing a Grand Slam event should require an almost unimaginable combination of skills and an unlikely ability to successfully tailor distinct approaches over a 5-month span. Thanks to better equipment, softer turf conditions, and parallel setups worldwide, contenders rarely have to change their games to fit a particular course or setup style. As the multiple components required to win a Grand Slam event are stripped away, creative and multidimensional players like Tiger Woods will have less chance to shine.

Diversity is out. Sameness is cool. Inexperience might even help a player.

In the interest of tradition, viewer appeal, and the overall perception of golf, the majors should at least require that players who dream of winning the "impregnable quadrilateral" make the same major-to-major adjustments that their predecessors had to endure.

WHERE RISK IS
NO LONGER REWARDING

*WHY CHANGES TO AUGUSTA NATIONAL HAVE
LITTLE IN COMMON WITH BOBBY JONES'S
VISION FOR HIS DREAM COURSE (AND WHY IT
COULD BE BAD FOR GOLF EVERYWHERE)*

The day after the 2002 Masters final round, CBS announcer Jim Nantz summed up the less-than-compelling concluding day: "We did not see the majestic moments that we expected."

Tiger Woods won the 2002 Masters with a cautious 71, as contenders Vijay Singh, Phil Mickelson, Ernie Els, and Retief Goosen struggled to register pars on the newly lengthened and narrowed Augusta National Golf Club.

"This is a course and a tournament that has always delivered the memorable shot, the heroic shot," Nantz said. "The only thing misleading about what I've just said is that Tiger didn't have it on full go because he didn't have to. He could have gone lower than 71, but he just had to play conservative. Once we got to 13, Tiger was going to win unless he tripped over the Hogan, Nelson, or Sarazen bridges."

Woods, whose record 18-under-par performance in 1997 may have unduly influenced the last 5 years of course design changes, summarized the new-look Augusta National.

"I think there's more risk than there is reward," he said.

Because planting trees, adding length, and narrowing fairways reduce options, the original flavor of Alister MacKenzie's co-design with club founder Bobby Jones has been lost. The departure in philosophy also seems to have reduced the number of potential Masters champions while making back-nine theatrics less likely.

Two-time Masters champion Ben Crenshaw believes that the addition of rough is "diametrically opposed to what Jones and MacKenzie had in mind."

A shared admiration for the Old Course at St. Andrews inspired MacKenzie and Jones's original concept of wide, undulating fairways that provided multiple ways to approach the complicated greens. Width allowed golfers of varying styles and abilities to adjust their tee shots depending on the day's hole location, the player's mood, or the ever-changing winds.

Jones wrote that the idea was "to reward the good shot by making the second shot simpler in proportion to the excellence of the first." The benefit of this seemingly vulnerable design scheme was Augusta National's ability to tempt the world's best players into heroic risk-taking, while luring less capable players into overaggressive and unwise shots.

"The course is not intended so much to punish the severely wayward shot as to reward adequately the stroke played with skill—and judgment," Jones wrote. "The perfect design should place a premium upon sound judgment as well as accurate striking by rewarding the correct placing of each shot."

Chairman Hootie Johnson has repeatedly stated that recent design changes restore a "premium on accuracy." His emphasis on rewarding the straightest path from tee to green differs from Jones's "correct placing of shots," which implied that players were given space to find their own route to the hole.

Even with its generous width, Augusta National was a deceptively difficult and complex layout because it presented so many tempting and viable options. Augusta wasn't interested in revealing who was best at hitting the ball consistently down the center and who could accumulate the most "greens in regulation."

"Here, we are playing all different kinds of shots," Woods said before the 2002 Masters and before seeing the latest changes. "We are playing bump-and-runs, we are playing high lobs, we are playing spinners and all different types of shots, which sometimes makes it even more diffi-cult, because of all your different options."

After watching several exciting Masters, Jones believed his design concept had been validated. During fast and firm Masters conditions, the options gave a variety of players a chance to win if they displayed intelligence, imagination, and an ability to cope with unexpected back-nine calamities.

"The finishes of the Masters Tournament have almost always been dramatic and exciting," Jones wrote. "It is my conviction that this has been the case because of the make-or-break quality of the second nine. This nine, with its abundant water hazards, each creating a perilous situation, can provide excruciating torture for the front-runner trying to hang on. Yet it can yield a very low score to the player making a closing rush."

Augusta National and consulting architect Tom Fazio insist that chang-es were necessary to counteract technology and the emerging wave of long-driving golfers currently in the collegiate ranks. In 1960, Bobby Jones expressed concern about such an approach.

"I believe it is true that with modern equipment and modern play-ers, we cannot make a golf course more difficult or more testing for the expert simply by adding length," Jones wrote. "The players of today are about as accurate with medium or long irons as with their pitching clubs. The only way to stir them up is by the introduction of subtleties around the greens."

"We are quite willing to have low scores made during the tournament. It is not our intention to rig the golf course so as to make it tricky. It is our feeling that there is something wrong with a golf course which will not yield a score in the sixties to a player who has played well enough to deserve it."

During 2002's final round, only Shigeki Maruyama broke 70 on a calm day when the rain-softened course might have been vulnerable in pre-vious years. The normally excitable Masters "patrons" were silenced by the succession of Sunday afternoon pars and bogies. 2003 saw Len Mattiace's epic final round 64. Certainly amazing, but he was the only one conquering the course. Again, mostly silence and light applause.

And more importantly, little tension created by the sense that the course was vulnerable to a charge.

In the Masters played since the par-5 fifteenth fairway was narrowed by a cluster of pines, the hole has yielded only four Sunday eagles through 2003. None of those eagles impacted the leader board.

The dramatic thirteenth also appears to have been transformed into a less vulnerable par 5. After yielding ten eagles in 2001, the newly lengthened hole gave up only four in 2002. No player registered an eagle during the final round in 2003.

The redesign work has been justified by the assertion that yearly course changes are as much a part of club lore as green jackets and Dwight Eisenhower.

"The modifications used to be more of one here, one there," Crenshaw said. "The additions were meant to be an improvement but they didn't necessarily mean much to the overall 18 holes. But these last couple of years have seen huge changes. Huge changes."

The extensive planting of trees to narrow the course may be the most extreme departure from Jones's philosophy, particularly considering his wish that Augusta National would reflect links-style golf.

"I don't see any need for a tree on a golf course," Jones once told journalist Alistair Cooke while the two sat on Jones's Augusta National cabin porch, looking out at the tenth hole.

Young trees have been transplanted within the taller pines to cut down on daring recovery shots. Jones, however, stated a preference for courses that allowed "the player to retrieve his situation."

Hootie Johnson denies that a fear of low scoring has anything to do with the changes. Or does he?

"We were not concerned with the scores, we never really gave that a lot of consideration," Johnson said during his 2002 press conference. "Of course, the short club, I guess leads to the score. We just hated that time after time, [players were] pulling out sand wedge or pitching wedge to par 4s."

Longtime Augusta chairman Clifford Roberts made his share of course changes, but resisted employing rough or excessive length to control scoring.

"It has been proven to our own satisfaction that those who patronize the Masters get more pleasure and excitement watching the great players make birdies than bogies," Roberts wrote in *The Story of Augusta National*. "Most assuredly, MacKenzie and Jones would have been disappointed if good scores by capable players had not been forthcoming."

Jones advocated a restricted competition ball in 1927. Might he insist on such a measure to return Augusta National to a strategic shotmakers' course, vulnerable to risk taking by a variety of players?

"I should never care to argue for anything which would lessen the difficulty of the game, for its difficulty is its greatest charm," Jones wrote. "But when, in spite of vast improvement in the ball, in seeking to preserve the difficulty and to make scoring as hard as it was in the old days, we make the mistake of destroying the effect of skill and judgment in an important department, I cannot help protesting."

STRADDLING THE CENTER LINE

". . . the true line to the hole should not always be the center of the fairway."
—Tom Simpson and H. N. Wethered

The "best" modern golf courses reward players who hit their balls down the middle. By surrounding our fairways with flanking hazards and rough in response to excessive driving distances, we now choose to favor the golfer who avoids "taking sides."

This has a nice metaphoric quality to it, don't you think?

After all, golf is a metaphor for life, or so they say.

It's fitting that the current fad is to confuse "accuracy" with straightness. The player who plods carefully down an imaginary center path, while straying neither right nor left, is not only accurate but also sure to be the best golfer. He is asked occasionally to make decisions, say, whether to use 3-wood or driver, or 2-versus 3-iron. But those are rarely significant decisions involving the qualities of temptation, risk assessment, or shot shaping. They are quantitative choices.

The center-line straddling recipe breeds success in politics, business, and most other areas these days. So why not in golf? Because golf is supposed to be fun, and there isn't much joy in trying to hug the center line with punishment looming if you should dare to slip off the center line.

Virtually every major since 1997 has featured belt-tightening, restrictive setups. Obedience golf. We've been told that the golf of yesteryear was somewhat more relaxed and less rigorous than our modern version, which is, of course, much more sound and manages to keep par relevant despite technology.

They're right, the center-line approach does quite often keep par relevant. But it chokes the life right out of golf.

Mike Weir won the 2003 Masters by playing the most error-free golf. Various writers, golf instructors, and golf experts immediately declared that the rough-surrounded fairways at Augusta National "now" provide a major championship test. "No longer" can the player bomb away, said Peter Kostis of CBS, USA Network, and Titleist.

See, no longer will those wild, side-taking tee shots and approaches be allowed. Let's revoke all those green jackets claimed on that free swinger's course!

The modern golf mentality subscribes to the idea that a course must dictate how and where you will go. The most subservient followers will be rewarded for their compliance. Walk that tightrope down the center, avoid trouble, evade risk, shun imagination, elude creativity, and don't be different. Comply to these demands, and you will be blessed with a big winner's check and an appearance on SportsCenter's "Sunday Night Conversation." You've been a good boy!

"Order has been restored," declared one television anchor after the new-look Masters kept players in line and made conformists out of the field.

Sadly, the ability to sidestep mines that were placed with little purpose is now commonly considered the measure of championship golf. It is a reaction to technology-fueled play that obsoletes and overwhelms architecture.

Oddly, the risk-taking and exceptional displays of talent that the Masters used to produce somehow had to be "fixed." How in the world did the Masters ever become such a revered event in the world of sport when it had such a flawed golf course all these years? Were we overtaken by azalea fumes? How did we let Nicklaus, Hogan, Snead, Palmer, Player, Watson, and Woods slip through the cracks?

The truth is, Augusta National or any other halfway decent design should not need rough if equipment was merely a means to demonstrate a player's skill. But now equipment provides the opportunity to overpower a course, so the knee-jerk response is to hinder power potential never seen before.

Augusta was created to be played without defined fairways. Even with many strange add-ons over the years, it has managed to retain its

2004: AUGUSTA NATIONAL LISTENS TO CRITICISM?

Early into the 2004 Masters week, much of the talk centered on just how boring the final round had become. Then Phil Mickelson, aided by Ernie Els, K. J. Choi, and others helped put that talk to rest with a sterling display of shotmaking and bold Sunday play that even longtime Masters observer Dan Jenkins called the greatest final round ever.

The players were helped by a brilliant final-round setup that allowed them to attack the hole locations for the first time in years. Perhaps Hootie Johnson and friends grew tired of press conference questions like this from early in the week:

> **Q:** "One of the things that they seem to lament the most is that it may take away from the back-nine charges of the past and people shooting 30s and scoring a lot of eagles and birdies and maybe more bogeys and doubles. Do you think that the character of the course has been changed from what it was in the past?"
>
> **Hootie Johnson:** "No. Well, it has been changed from what it was, thank goodness. They would be driving 17, and Tiger Woods almost drove 18 the last time he won. The changes were necessary and appropriate."

brilliance thanks to its green complexes. They still demanded accuracy, but of a different kind. Accuracy of the mind.

Add some rough with those new little pine trees and some excessively lengthened holes, and Augusta rarely asks the golfer, as Max Behr said, to take "immediate risks" if he wishes "to rid himself of future liabilities."

Old Augusta, and strategic courses like it, rewarded planning and calculated risks that put risk takers in a better position than the folks who took the safe route. The design turned out just as Bobby Jones hoped. He wanted a course of "a democratic nature," as Ben Crenshaw called it.

It wasn't all good news for the Masters, as Mickelson's epic win was television's lowest-rated Masters final round since 1993, when Bernhard Langer won by four shots. Masters ratings were down 12 percent from 2003 when 1 million more people watched Mike Weir and Len Mattiace finish in a playoff.

Sports columnist Christine Brennan wrote the following in *USA Today*:

> It is not good news for the world of golf that a gem of a finish such as this one was rewarded with only a slightly larger audience than the one that gathered around TV sets to watch Langer win his second Masters 11 years ago. What this tells us about the popularity of golf is that it's still all about Tiger Woods. Tiger brings grandmothers to their TV sets. Phil brings golf nuts. And because golf is a niche sport, with its devoted, insular, and wealthy following, it's never going to be the mainstream American sport that football, baseball or basketball are.

Still, the Masters was restored to its former glory and fans can only hope that a lesson was learned.

By asking the golfer to calculate future liabilities before attacking the hole, we compel the player to be both physically and mentally alert. The use of rigging devices is nothing more than a ploy to keep golfers conforming and obeying. But is that why people take up golf? To take orders from an architect or committee setting up a course?

Simply appreciating tradition won't reverse this dreadful trend. It will have to change when the numbers come in, perhaps through a message via the Nielson group: Your ratings are plummeting, no one wants to watch this grind.

Or word from the accountants: Your rounds are down.

Maybe it'll be the bad news from Wall Street that wakes people up to the dangers of narrow golf: Spending is down, growth is out—sell, sell, sell!

Golf is a metaphor for life.

SUCCUMBING TO DUMBING?

(WHY TIGER WILL HAVE A HARD TIME WINNING MORE MAJORS THAN JACK)

"Well, it's right there in front of you. I've always liked golf courses that are the old-school style, tree-lined fairways and the fairways are well-defined. There's no surprises about this golf course. That's one of the great things about coming here, is we don't get the chance to play golf courses of this type very often. I mean, it's certainly a thrill for me to come back and play a golf course that I really love, but more importantly, to sit up there and just see shots. Every hole is just well defined for you, just get up there and hit the shot."
— TIGER WOODS, ON FIRESTONE GOLF CLUB–SOUTH

That's Tiger after the first round of the 2003 World Championship event. Those are the big-money tournaments no one really cares about because they were created to prevent Greg Norman from starting a world tour.

The best and most imaginative player of our generation says a course is great because it's all "right there in front of you." There's no imagination required, no study necessary. For a player like Tiger, who once thrived on cerebral golf courses that require study and creativity to conquer, his comments reveal an odd transformation.

When such a creative and intelligent player embraces bland, surprise-free, intelligence-free architecture, what can you do? Complain!

I understand that when you are playing for a lot of money, blind shots are a pain, gusts of wind cause you to back off, and inconsistent green firmness can be frustrating. And I know it's really a pain to have to play a practice round and note which greens are firmer than others, or to have to figure out how to gauge a shot that isn't entirely visible, or to devise some oddly shaped shot to get close to a particular day's hole location. Those things require thought, a big no-no in golf today.

Still, how is it a good thing when everything on a golf course "is right in front of you"? Is there any mental challenge to stepping on the tee and knowing exactly how you should play each of the eighteen holes? We're already giving out yardages and pin sheets, does the architecture have to hold the player's hand, too?

It used to be that the shrewd golfer was rewarded for adapting to surprises or picking up local knowledge. The creative player used his ingenuity to come up with original shots to solve unexpected problems.

That's what was so refreshing and marvelous about Tiger Woods. He was a throwback in the mold of Jones, Hogan, and Nicklaus, the all-time, megachampions that he promised to equal or even exceed. He still could end up bettering them, but if predictable course setups continue, he needs a lot of good luck: Talent, imagination, and determination won't be enough.

Tiger liked to pull off wacky shots and do things no one in modern times had seen since the era of Nicklaus, Trevino, and Watson. He seemed to embrace surprises and appeared to enjoy crafting ways out of situations that less resilient players found annoying and perplexing. He could visualize a shot that was not defined for him. Often, Tiger executed bold shots that other players couldn't quite imagine, or if they could, they wouldn't dare try to pull them off.

Tiger would dare and usually perform in amazing fashion. And he also seemed to know when *not* to take chances.

Maybe Tiger-proofing has worked. It sounds as if he's signed on to the plodding, thought-free, sterile modern game that will make it hard for him to win more majors than Jack Nicklaus.

Based on Tiger's recent comments and compared with the a miration he displayed just a few years ago for the spontan ity of links golf, Tiger has somehow forgotten that his advantage was on a golf course that didn't tell the player exactly what to do—a design that required intelligence, creativity, and a little curiosity.

The bad news for Tiger is that Jones and Nicklaus never reached the point of embracing shallow designs. Jones criticized predictable American courses when he was in his prime competitive years, and was even more critical as he got older. Nicklaus always understood that a course that rewarded creativity and decision-making would give him an advantage over other similarly talented ball strikers and putters.

Father Earl, I know you're busy with the foundation and raising $25 million for the practice center in Anaheim. But your son needs a little reminder of what type of golf course separates him from all the merely really outstanding players. Hint: It's the kind of architecture that requires the player to think, adapt, and work, not the kind where "every hole is just well defined for you" so you can "just get up there and hit the shot."

THE LOST POTENTIAL
OF THE TPC'S

"The idea of stadium golf, in which courses are designed to give greater accessibility to the fans and provide unrestricted views of tee shots, fairway shots, and putts, is a tremendous innovation. The master plan went awry, however, when so many of the TPCs were designed as target golf courses."

—PETER JACOBSEN

One of the best things you can say about the PGA Tour's Tournament Players Club (TPC) facilities is that they may be the only tour-related division that hasn't yet allied itself with "branding" corporate "partners." Meaning, there is still no TPC at Viagra Village. No TPC at Propecia Beach.

Wait, there is the TPC at Deere Run, an ode to the nearby John Deere Company, who just happens to sponsor a tournament there. At least it's a subtle reference.

Frankly, the tour can do whatever it wants to milk money out of the TPCs, but for viewers and fans of golf, the TPCs are a failure. Many are tough to walk, lack interesting architecture, and sometimes are nothing more than a housing development endorsed by the PGA Tour.

If they insist on building more TPCs, the tour might try to learn from the few good ones they have by focusing on architecture that creates excitement for the overall good of golf.

The concept of the Tournament Players Club would have actually been a good one if it had been carried out with a diverse, architecture-focused master plan. Stadium mounding provides a much better vantage point for spectators to watch the action, especially in a sport where spectating is hard work. And the tour has always needed an infusion of interesting designs to make the golf more attractive to television viewers and spectators.

PARITY IS COOL

Tiger has something else working against him.

Many folks are comforted by parity. Call it an offshoot of political correctness or our conformity culture, but for some odd reason parity is cool.

Before Tiger Woods turned pro in 1997, we had heard for years that there would never be another dominant player.

Woods came along and dominated from 1997 to 2002, winning eight majors. Then Tiger had an average year in 2003 and still won player of the year.

Near the end of 2003, many players and even the commissioner raved that the tour was so much more competitive and how great that was for golf. New stars were born and it wasn't all about Tiger.

Of course, privately, they are rooting for Tiger to play as much as he can and win as often as possible because the next television contract still needs Woods and his automatic 2-point Nielson boost.

But Tiger, in your quest to be the best ever, you will have to overcome not only course setups that discourage heroic play while rewarding the week's best plodder and putter, but also the mind-set that celebrates progressive technology's ability to aid lesser players to compete with you and other top players.

Continued on next page

However, TPCs have gone consistently wrong on the architectural side of things. Instead of creating a variety of courses with distinct design characteristics, the PGA Tour has an in-house design team that handled most of the projects carried out over the last few years. They slapped on a "player consultant" for good measure, assuming this formula would give them a variety of designs. Instead, they have mostly straightforward (i.e., dull) target golf courses that all look pretty much the same; a couple are downright hideous (Valencia, Heron Bay).

"Tiger should be more outspoken about it because it has hurt him more than anyone else," Nick Price said. "There is nothing wrong with the equipment he is using, believe me, but he has lost his edge because the guys have equipment that has helped them catch up to him."

Consider this December 14, 2003, article from the *New York Times Magazine*, which celebrated the new PGA Tour driver-testing device as one of the better inventions of the year:

> While golf's big names were quibbling this summer with metallurgists and tape measures, every one of the major tournaments was won by a relative unknown, none of them particularly big hitters by today's elongated standard. They're merely where Tiger was just a few years ago, and that, it turns out, is plenty far enough. With so many golfers now reaching places on the fairway that used to be attainable only by the likes of Tiger and John Daly, golf has all of a sudden opened up again, and the leader boards are often full of surprises.

Remember, Tiger, parity is cool, especially when the playing field is leveled by outside forces like technology or course setup committees.

Part of the problem is that "player-architects" on the design team know that their tour colleagues will be playing their design work. So player-consultant suggestions revolve around sterilizing features and making every hole as "fair" as possible. This results in very few of the classic do-or-die holes that make golf fun to watch.

Thankfully, there are three anomalies. Perhaps the tour will make the connection between architecture and the compelling finishes that take place at these TPCs nearly every year.

The TPCs at Scottsdale (Arizona, Tom Weiskopf/Jay Morrish design), Sawgrass (Florida, Pete Dye design), and River Highlands (Connecticut, Bobby Weed redesign of Pete Dye) have proven to be excellent tests of golf. Each presents a solid set of holes that not only brings out the best in the players, but also creates entertaining tournaments.

What makes them different?

Each is highlighted by short par 4s and tempting par 5s on the home stretch. The driveable par-4 fifteenth at River Highlands has become one of most memorable holes on the tour, as has the driveable two-shot seventeenth at Scottsdale. Both include water and all sorts of agonizing decisions to make. Galleries have unobstructed views and often can watch action on more than one hole. Noise reverberates throughout the course (at least at those not split up by houses). And voila, atmosphere is created!

Shorter risk-reward holes make viewing fun because we finally get to see the best players in the world struggle the way they should—having to make on-the-spot judgment calls that force deviation from their game plans. You find out who the best players are when this type of challenge is presented by the architect.

It took years for the TPC at Sawgrass to go from a freakish design to the respected layout it is now. Fine-tuning has made it one of the better designs on the tour despite some pathetic changes in the course's cosmetics (wannabe Augusta azaleas, blinding white bunkers, and U.S. Open rough).

To produce the kind of memorable golf many of us hope to witness, the TPC concept needs to be approached more carefully. Courses must have more time to mature before they host the best players in the world, but more importantly, they need to be designed with attention to detail. The PGA Tour must become more imaginative so that the "TPC brand" symbolizes more than it does now, which is, for the most part, mediocrity and drab tournament viewing.

THE BUNKER, R.I.P.?

"Sure, I was angry at the time. I would say it's getting to be a little bit more of a habit out here with some of the caddies—not finishing the job so to speak. There is an art to raking a bunker, you just don't slop the rake around in there."

—JEFF MAGGERT, AFTER ENDING UP IN A
RAKE MARK DURING THE 2003 MASTERS FINAL ROUND

The golf professional and single-digit players have won the battle. They have declared that the bunker must be fair. When in the sand, a.k.a. a hazard, they must have a good lie at all times. The average golfer concurs because who can ever forget that awful "fried egg" that cost them a match in the Watts Gunn Flight of the Mayflower Cup.

Thus, the golf course superintendent must do everything in his power to take the danger out of the sand, to the point of wasting countless man hours primping sand and ultimately rendering the bunker decorative but useless.

How did the bunker transmogrify into a paradoxical joke?

The answer lies deep in the rough.

The championship and even regular day golf mentality is that rough is essential to "defend" a golf course. Some even believe rough has always been part of golf.

And we all know that everyday committees worship what they see on television, so as rough has become more prevalent, the bunker has developed into a more appealing place for a ball to rest. Throw in the 60-degree wedge, and the bunker becomes even more useless as a hazard. Either way, the golf course superintendent is pressured by clients and self-important tournament competitors to convert these hazards into areas nearly as attractive as the fairway.

The role of the bunker hit an epic low when an on-course announcer gasped that Tiger Woods and Bob May both drew tough lies on the tenth hole at Valhalla, simply because the bottom of the bunker was not flat. Perfectly raked. But not flat.

The announcer pointed out the injustice even after one of his colleagues had spent the previous 5 minutes telling us that the players aim for the tenth hole front bunker. Why? In order to have the best chance to get up and down for birdie!

Instead of a place to avoid, the high-rough setup made that bunker the best place from which to make birdie. Flat lie or not. The Nicklaus-designed hazard, created as a place of danger for those taking a risky avenue to the hole, graduated to being the primary lay-up area on a par 5.

Like most others today, that particular bunker's role was altered largely because of the nasty new rough around the green. To compensate for the severity of rough, the course setup gurus ordered that the bunkers be raked in a way that would promote "fair" golf.

Of course, we don't need to go so far as to copy Oakmont's homemade furrowing rakes because they discourage any kind of recovery. But the governing bodies can stop insisting on hideous rough. They can also stop emphasizing manicured raking and start subtly returning some teeth to the bunker by making the sand fluffy enough to cause a player to think twice about laying up in one. The sand can still be reasonable enough that a talented golfer will pull off a skillful recovery from time to time.

I'd love to see a tour event played on a fast, roughless golf course where the bunkers are nasty. Perhaps the bunkers could be raked Wednesday morning before the Pro-Am, but left untouched the rest of the week unless there's a harsh storm. (Well, not even then!) Take the rakes away, and let the players take care of the sand. And keep the grass short in the immediate area so bunkers and their surrounds will become places to avoid. The short grass will also siphon more balls into the sand. Imagine that!

Some prominent golf organization will have to start a trend by no longer letting the players dictate the setup. Maybe it'll be a European tour event or an unofficial "silly season" event, or maybe Tiger will say this is how hazards should be, and that'll do it. But someone has to return menace to the bunker. Otherwise, the sporting spirit of golf will be permanently lost.

THE (LOST?) ART OF COURSE SETUP

TIGER-PROOFING GONE BAD

"They give us a pin sheet at the beginning of every round. In 21 years I have never seen 3 feet from the right or left edge. I have seen it five or six times this year already. There is a whole different mentality going on in this game right now, and I'm not sure it's good for the game. I'm not sure that tricking all this stuff up to try to combat [distance] is the way to do things."

—HAL SUTTON, 2003

Midway through the first round of the 2002 Australian Open, play was cancelled because Victoria Golf Club's greens were too fast. Putts hit past some of the holes actually trickled back short of the cup. Of the twenty-seven players who finished eighteen holes, none was under par on a mild day with light winds. This setup folly prompted New Zealand's Greg Turner to remark, "It's not the incompetence that astounds me, just the extent of it."

The rash of course setup foibles worldwide—most notably questionable ploys at the last six U.S. Opens—has many wondering what is causing the wave of embarrassments. Has this been happening all along and we simply didn't notice until the Tiger Woods era of media scrutiny? Are these maladies a result of governing bodies rigging tournament courses to mask ineffective equipment regulation? Or are they simply a result of incompetence?

As far back as the 1920s, writer Bernard Darwin questioned the introduction of "rough" and other course setup tricks. Because of his love for the natural, unfettered Old Course at St. Andrews, Darwin expressed concern about the effect of restrictive course setups on architecture, on speed of play, and on everyday golf. Architectural styles were already changing after professionals like J. H. Taylor and Harold Hilton complained about center-line fairway bunkers and other features they deemed unfair.

Bobby Jones's authority and eloquence forced all of golf to take notice when he commented on setup issues. Though he expressed displeasure only occasionally during his competitive years, Jones did not hide his disapproval of the 1925 U.S. Open setup where Oakmont's bunkers had been prepared with deep-furrowing rakes. In later years, he wrote of his disdain for over-watered courses.

According to longtime USGA executive director Frank Hannigan, the United States Golf Association took control of U.S. Open course setup in 1952. USGA president Richard Tufts and executive director Joe Dey stepped in after what Hannigan said was a "hugely erratic" run of setups handled by host courses and their superintendents. The inconsistencies boiled over during the infamous 1951 Oakland Hills U.S. Open, which prompted eleven-time major championship winner Walter Hagen to utter his now legendary grievance that "the course was playing the players, not the players playing the course."

The USGA setup pattern has been simple: narrow, rough-lined fairways that reward straight tee shots. Add in firm greens surrounded by nasty rough and place a premium on greens hit in regulation. Pars are well earned.

The effort to protect the mysterious "integrity" of par and emphasize straight drives over strategically placed tee shots has muted the role of strategic course architecture. In addition to the not-so-popular tradition of changing par 5s to par 4s to reduce the number of red numbers posted, there have been high-rough and concrete green setups that pushed the limits of reason. An extreme example was 1974's "massacre at Winged Foot," where Hale Irwin's 7-over-par was good enough to win by two strokes.

In 1979 a bizarre overnight spruce-planting was intended to prevent Lon Hinkle from shortcutting a hole by playing down one of Inverness's parallel fairways. There also have been rumors of last-minute Gibberrelic acid applications to stimulate immediate rough growth. Though these antics illustrate the more obvious USGA ploys, outcomes seldom seemed greatly tainted by such measures.

The 1980s featured consistent setups spearheaded by longtime USGA staff member P. J. Boatwright, who mastered the art of a "tough-but-fair" U.S. Open. He was succeeded by his protégé, longtime amateur great and current Champions Tour player David Eger. In a minor departure from the previous USGA philosophy, former president Sandy Tatum encouraged Eger to introduce chipping areas around certain greens at Shinnecock Hills, Baltusrol, and Pebble Beach. This encouraged more aggressive approach shots while creating options for recovery play.

After Eger left to work for the PGA Tour, USGA championship setups were handled by rules and competitions director Tom Meeks, executive director David Fay, chairs of the championship committee, and championship agronomist Tim Moraghan, with input from a USGA-endorsed "Open doctor."

U.S. Open setups continued to reflect the legacy of Boatwright and Eger until the 1998 event at Olympic Club, where extreme measures backfired disastrously during play. According to Hannigan, the recent miscues have been "odd and isolated but legitimate attention getters."

Olympic's slender 18th green featured a second round rear hole location cut into a slope earmarked as questionable in pre-tournament evaluations. Payne Stewart fans will never forget that sunny Friday afternoon when his short par putt lipped out, leaving the two-time Open champion to stand in shock, arms folded, watching his ball trickle down the green. Stewart faced a 25-footer for bogey.

But the Friday antics were only part of a strange week in which many players felt the USGA employed setup tactics to compensate for Olympic's short (by modern standards) length.

"The course had lost much of its character by Thursday," says Eger, who qualified for the 1998 Open. "It had been dried out to the extent that it was virtually impossible for tee shots to come to rest in some of the sloping fairways. Great courses like Olympic, Shinnecock, and Pinehurst #2 should be played as their designers meant them to be. They should be, if anything, enhanced during the Open, not disguised by unreasonably narrow fairways, overly penal rough, rock hard turf, and poor cup placements."

The following year at Pinehurst #2, the USGA admirably refused to grow rough around Donald Ross's famed crowned greens while also featuring shorter than usual fairway rough. Players praised the setup until they saw tournament hole locations perched precariously close to the putting surface edges. With Open speeds kicking in, a weekend disaster was avoided only because of the un-June-like clouds and drizzle.

"They expanded the greens and ended up putting half the pins on the roll-offs," writes Jack Nicklaus in his book, *Nicklaus by Design*. "That was never part of Donald Ross's vision—the USGA was just trying to find more ways to counter the ball."

In 2000, Pebble Beach introduced the widely criticized second-hole par switch. A par 5, reachable in two for long drivers in previous Opens, the second hole was considered too short by modern three-shot standards and changed to a long par 4. Less talked about, but still obvious, were the well-watered green approaches and bone-dry putting surfaces. Both peculiar setup elements were forgotten after Tiger Woods's epic runaway victory.

The 2001 U.S. Open at Southern Hills featured another first: greens too fast for play. Early-week practice rounds revealed that the newly resurfaced ninth and eighteenth greens were so slick that balls hit to the middle of the putting surface rolled back off the greens and down into the fairway below. The USGA raised mowing heights, leaving the new bent grass lumpy and leafier than on the other sixteen surfaces. By Sunday afternoon, putting fiascos by leaders Mark Brooks, Stewart Cink, and Retief Goosen affected the outcome.

At Bethpage in 2002, the 490-yard tenth hole featured the now- infamous 250-yard forced carry over high rough to a fairway that proved unreachable for most of the field when wind and rain showed up in round two. Just as controversial was the fairway contour design for the Black Course's 499-yard par-4 twelfth. USGA officials provided just 12 paces of fairway width for those driving 260–270 yards. But, if a player carried the left-side bunker and a patch of dense rough with a 285-yard drive, the fairway expanded to 26 paces wide.

"What were they thinking?" Nick Price asked of the setup on the two par 4s. "It defies logic."

Overseas, the Royal and Ancient Golf Club of St. Andrews would like to forget the 1999 British Open at Carnoustie, perhaps the textbook course setup debacle. The oddness was not confined to one hole or to a single poor decision. Instead, ultra-narrow fairways accented with fertilized rough and defended by an unapologetic superintendent made the classic Carnoustie links almost unrecognizable. A design that would have held its own without *any* pretournament preparations became a peculiar battle zone of forgettable golf, capped off by Jean Van DeVelde's unforgettable attempt to reach the eighteenth hole.

Some have lamented the British Open's shift to irrigated fairways and narrow fairways that restrict the driver. Authentic links characteristics once provided a refreshing contrast to the lush, inland, precision-guided U.S. Open. However, Muirfield's slender fairways were widely praised during the 2002 British Open, because players felt that the long hitter's advantage had been reduced. Others pointed out that the tightly bunched field never did fully separate itself, and a bizarre four-man playoff ensued.

"I have been disappointed to see so many players hitting irons off the tee," said Peter Alliss before Sunday's final round where eventual winner Ernie Els drove with a long iron all day. "Maybe they should narrow the fairways and widen them further up so that it tempts people to use a driver. Driving used to be a great skill, a real weapon in your armory."

Not long ago, only a few traditionalists pointed out that these extreme setups were created to mask the lack of technology regulation. They have now been joined by golf's all-time greatest player.

"The long ball has a negative effect on tournament setups," says Nicklaus. "It forces tournament committees to protect par in some way, and what they'll generally do is put the pins in more awkward positions. It's no longer a question of protecting par, it's a question of protecting the golf course. The golfers are probably better today. Equipment is better. The golf ball goes farther. So they shoot lower scores, so what? I don't have a problem with that. The only problem I have is when none of the difficulty ever comes into play."

Architect Brian Silva agrees that most classic architecture is overmatched in today's game.

"Tournament setups have favored laser-assisted straight fairways, rather than allowing fairways to twist and turn on their way from tee to green," says Silva, whose design partner Mark Mungeam directed the renovation of 2003 U.S. Open site Olympia Fields. "Ultra narrow fairways, deep and penalizing rough, and Stimpmeter speeds way too fast for green slopes developed during the Golden Age have exerted an artificial 'brake' on golf scores, keeping the spotlight off of how far the golf ball has been traveling."

In 1992, tour player David Feherty voiced his concern about newly tightened fairways and excessive rough designed to protect par. "I'm always hearing that it's good when par is relevant," Feherty wrote. "I agree, but if athletes swim the 200-meter freestyle faster than they did 10 years ago, they don't throw Jell-O in the pool."

Greg Norman recently pointed out that the length-driven setup gimmicks eliminate options, and technology breeds a less complete player. "Anyone who believes the game of golf in America hasn't become one-dimensional should study closely what has occurred with the best players in the world in this year's major championships," Norman wrote in 2002. "Technology—including golf balls that don't spin as they did, square grooves, graphite shafts with virtually no torque, and lob wedges with 62 degrees of loft or more—have stolen the ability of many of today's young players to adapt under changing conditions. Strategically placed bunkers, hanging lies, and challenging turning points are what will put the teeth back into championship golf, not 500-yard par 4s."

In light of unthinkable driving distances and vastly improved course conditioning, is there any way to present challenging championship golf on courses of reasonable length, without turning majors into freak shows?

"I'm sorry, they didn't get a grip on the manufacturers," Hal Sutton said after seeing the USGA–supported design changes to Riviera Country Club. "And now they are trying to make it up by changing the greatest pieces of art work that we have in the world. I think that they went about this all wrong. Meaning the USGA should have stopped this before it [ever got] to this point, instead of changing great golf courses."

A SETUP FOR THE AGES:
SHINNECOCK HILLS 2004

"So long, old pal. It's been nice to know you, U.S. Open."
—James Achenbach, *Golfweek*

Johnny Miller concluded NBC's 2003 U.S. Open telecast by saying that Olympia Fields was a bit too tame by USGA standards. He warned that players had better look out because the USGA would exact revenge at Shinnecock Hills.

Miller was right. Sort of. Though he probably couldn't imagine the bureaucratic unraveling that took place.

Unlike the debacle at Carnoustie in 1999, the setup for Shinnecock Hills started off fine. But a star-studded leaderboard got to 6-under-par after the opening thirty-six holes. And then the USGA seemingly lost control.

According to several witnesses, Shinnecock's steeply pitched "Redan" seventh green was double cut and rolled Friday night under USGA supervision. It was part of the setup plan all week to toughen up the course for weekend play.

Saturday morning, a knowledgeable Shinnecock staff member invited to watch the daily setup warned the USGA staff that the forecasted northwest wind might make things precarious. Still, nothing was done to prepare the seventh for the possibility of extreme conditions.

During Open week, only volunteer superintendents from noted courses across America were assigned the sensitive tasks of rolling or mowing greens. Still, this was the USGA's course for the week. They rented it and superintendent Mark Michaud's maintenance crew was there to follow orders, many of which were carried out under USGA staff or Championship committee supervision.

As Saturday's round developed and the course dried out, it soon became apparent that few players could hold the seventh green. Worse, many chip shots were hit to the hole, only to have them roll back off the green. USGA executive director David Fay joked during the telecast that the seventh was the "toughest par 4 in America."

But as the day wore on and leader Phil Mickelson made double bogey there (he later lost the tournament by two strokes), Fay chimed in from his NBC announcer position. He said it had been "brought to our attention" that the seventh green was "by mistake, rolled this morning."

Fay said this as cameras showed workers beginning to mow the green after Saturday's round.

It was one thing if Fay received bad information. But to pass off the story as a "mistake" as the green was being double cut (at a tenth of an inch!), displayed an unprecedented lack of foresight by the well-paid executive director.

Many watching at home were asking the question that no one at NBC bothered to pose: If the green became unplayable after one rolling, why are you out double cutting the green, which is, in essence, another rolling (mowers have heavy rollers on them)?

The director of rules and competitions, Tom Meeks, is normally the USGA man out front in charge of the course setup. Yet he made just a few appearances on the Golf Channel and ESPN, with executive committee member Walter Driver dealing with the rest of the press. Fay was nowhere to be seen.

Driver displayed why executive committee members have historically never been too visible at the Open. Despite preparation sessions with pricey public relations firm Powell-Tate, he offered up reasoning that could not have been true.

"I'm sure someone was asked to roll [the seventh green], but that instruction came from someone down the chain of command, and I don't know who," Driver said. "I think it's just human error. I think somebody thought they were supposed to roll it and told the fellow who was on the rolling machine to go ahead. He didn't just make it up, but it didn't come from me."

MEDIA PILE ON

These clippings will not be featured in the USGA's 2004 annual report.

Frank Beard on *SI.com*: "There was a time when winning one of the greatest championships in the world by the best players of the day was the focus of the U.S. Open. Today, that focus has changed to showcasing the arrogant elitism of the USGA and its total disregard for providing a challenging but fair and fun golf course."

Steve Elling in the *Orlando Sentinel*: "the U.S. Golf Association blew it in a big way, in terms of competence, obstinance, and accountability."

James Achenbach in *Golfweek*: "Contemporary golf is out of balance. Because the best golfers now hit the ball so far and straight, and because today's fairways are so firm and fast, the final safeguard against low scores has been invoked—rock-hard greens with inaccessible pin positions. There is a great danger in this strategy, because it can make most of the competitors look silly. Worse yet, it can embarrass the game of golf."

After the event, none of the green "rollers" wanted to go on the record for fear of losing their real jobs or jeopardizing USGA events at their home courses. But each of the four working the rolling machines denied Driver's account of a mistaken rolling. The USGA later sent a letter to the club apologizing for any insinuation that the staff or volunteers did anything wrong. The USGA's letter was not made public.

Shinnecock Hills got out of hand under USGA orders and supervision, yet for the first time ever, the USGA reacted to an obviously embarrassing situation by blaming someone else for something that never happened, while concocting a farcical excuse of a "mistaken rolling."

Frank Hannigan likened the USGA spin to "saying Sauchiehall Street was inadvertently torn up overnight."

Sadly, the antics had only begun that sunny Saturday afternoon.

He also wrote, "the Open I know and love seems to be gone, replaced by some imposter."

Tod Leonard in the *San Diego Union-Tribune*: "Look, we all enjoy occasionally seeing professional golfers bumble around like weekend hackers. It makes us feel good. It reaffirms just how maddeningly difficult golf really is. But the U.S. Open shouldn't be like playing the volcano holes at Boomers."

Craig Dolch in the *Palm Beach Post*: "The USGA just doesn't get it."

David Davies in *The Guardian*, London: "It is a terrible indictment of those responsible for setting up the course that only 18.2% managed to hit the seventh green on Sunday, only 19.7% hit the short second, and only 21.2% hit the par-4 tenth."

Most prominent of all, **Thomas Boswell** wrote in the *Washington Post* that it was "a day of almost hallucinatory golf embarrassments. In golf terms, that USGA decision qualifies as a mental quadruple-bogey, a veritable snowman of bone-headedness."

High winds blew into the wee hours Saturday night. During the early evening hours the wind was already howling, so The Golf Channel's Rich Lerner asked Tom Meeks if the USGA planned to put some water on the course to keep it from getting any drier. Meeks said no.

The old Shinnecock irrigation system was too weak to combat the wind, so the system was not used to maintaining some balance between fast and out of control. The wind would have just blown the water away.

However, Sunday morning was another story. Even with the previous day's fiasco, the first group of Kevin Stadler and J. J. Henry posted a pair of triple-bogies on the seventh hole. The next group through posted a triple-bogey and a double-bogey. NBC's Johnny Miller grimly stated that the hole was "unplayable."

After those two groups, the USGA halted play on the seventh after those two groups and applied a light misting to keep balls from rolling off the surface. Just a few sprinklings of water proved that they could keep greens playable. But the USGA waited until it was a certified disaster on the seventh to act.

Perhaps because they still didn't believe this was their fault.

Dropping by the NBC booth Sunday morning to soak up feel-good vibes following a puff-piece where he was seen high-fiving underprivileged youth during a staged photo-op clinic, USGA president Fred Ridley defended the seventh hole-debacle, saying it was caused by a "perfect storm" of wind, sun, hole location, and the accidental rolling that never happened.

When NBC's Dan Hicks joked that they'd gone from talking about growing the game to growing grass, Ridley didn't laugh. Instead, he looked down and NBC moved on. Thankfully, he didn't launch into a standard USGA defense: They all had to play it.

That job went to championship committee head Walter Driver, who wheeled out the classic excuse invoked when other setups have gone over the top. "I would rather not have had the controversy, but we couldn't do anything about it," Driver said. "You know, you can't be disappointed in something that you can't completely control."

"Well, there's a great quote from Sandy Tatum, one of our predecessors, as the president of the USGA. We weren't trying to humiliate the best players in the world, we were trying to identify them."

Yet as Sunday's round progressed it became clear that the USGA was humiliating both the players and themselves. Soon after the seventh-hole debacle, hose crews were called in to douse emerging hotspots throughout the course. This simple act should have occurred before the start of Sunday play. Why did it require actual competition to show that the conditions needed to be subdued to get through the day?

The par-4 tenth averaged 5.03 the last day thanks to an unholdable green. Twenty-eight scores were posted in the 80s. No one broke par for the day. If Retief Goosen (twenty-four putts) and Phil Mickelson do not hole out from just about everywhere, the day is a total disaster because any significant afternoon wind makes the course unplayable. This would have resulted in a suspension of play and an unfathomable Monday finish.

Is all of this living-on-the-edge worth risking the suspension of play, or worth the embarrassment?

Apparently so, as the USGA continues the trend of pushing the Open over the edge to protect par and mask technology-driven changes in the game that overwhelm classic courses like Shinnecock Hills.

All week, the 400-yard first hole was a driver and sand-wedge for most players. Daniel Chopra had 27 yards to the hole Sunday. The par-5 sixteenth, considered one of the hardest par 5s in the world when previous Opens were staged at Shinnecock, became a potential eagle hole down the stretch.

Sadly, the course is overwhelmed in today's professional game unless you resort to extremes. If the USGA merely tried to keep the course setup similar to the first two days with perhaps tougher hole locations for the weekend, the winner might have reached 10, even 12 under par.

Would that taint the championship more than the fiasco that took place?

"I really felt after Friday that they were going to let this happen to the golf course," said third-place finisher Jeff Maggert. "They look up at the scoreboard and they see all those red numbers and they panic. They don't want 10 under to win their tournament, and that's just the philosophy that they've had forever."

Those calling the shots at the USGA continue to believe that low scoring reflects poorly on them. Some might call this stupidity, others would label it narcissism of the worst kind. After all, isn't the U.S. Open about the players instead of the people running it?

Tiger Woods said, "It's our national championship and they lost control of the golf course. There's nothing wrong with guys being under par."

"They've done it again," contestant Jerry Kelly said. "They've topped themselves. When are they going to grow a head? [They should] get off their high horse and be good to the game. It's an ego contest. . . . I think they're ruining golf. Period."

And Tom Kite summed it up best.

"I think that's the only defense right now," Kite said of the setup. "They've lost the war with equipment. The players are bigger, faster, stronger. And so they're hitting the ball so far that length means nothing. You can make a golf course 8,000 yards and water it down to where the ball plugs and somebody will still be able to reach the green and do some nice stuff. I love the U.S. Open. I really do. I think our national championship is the premier event in golf. It's a shame when they push the golf course to the limit as much as they have in this particular case."

After the U.S. Open, USGA executive director David Fay acknowledged that in an "attempt to set the course very difficult, in this attempt to get the course near the edge, we went over the edge," Fay told a radio talk show guest-hosted by journalist John Feinstein. "It was not by design. It quickly got away from us."

However, at the 2004 British Open where players and media raved about Royal Troon's setup, the man in charge of the Shinnecock setup ran into more trouble when comments he made to the *Boston Globe* surfaced. The USGA's Tom Meeks, apparently having watched a different U.S. Open, said that "a lot of golfers lost their patience and gave up early in the round. I really think Ernie Els gave up after the first hole."

Els responded angrily. "How do you give up? That is the most ridiculous thing I've ever heard in my life. I've never given up on any round of golf in my life. If I did give up, I would have shot 100."

"You know what? They have got no idea," Els continued. "To take one of the best golf courses in this entire world and to make it a farce like that, they've got egg on their face."

Meeks apologized, relaying to the media that, "I just said, 'Ernie, I was wrong. I shouldn't have said that.' I explained to him it was just a casual remark. And it was just my opinion."

It was just his opinion. He shouldn't have said that. Does that mean he still thinks Els gave up?

The 2004 U.S. Open marked an all-time low for the USGA. They concocted a setup for the ages in the name of protecting par and masking the real problem: Inefficient USGA equipment regulation has thrown the professional game out of whack.

MORE PROGRESS: SLOW PLAY

"By the time you get to your ball, if you don't know what to do with it, try another sport."

—JULIUS BOROS

Compounding the silliness of narrowing and lengthening courses, the impact of unregulated technology is exacerbating modern golf's slow-play problem.

In 2003 the PGA Tour instituted a new set of guidelines and fines for players "put on the clock" too many times. The tour practically jumped for joy when the average 2003 round sped up by 10 minutes, to, get this, just 4 hours and 37 minutes.

What progress.

The best players in the world take over 4½ hours on immaculately groomed courses with no lost balls. Meanwhile course operators ask everyday golfers to do it in less time, without caddies to carry bags and marshals to locate errant balls.

Respected PGA Tour rules official Mark Russell declined to identify one player who was fined for slow play and offered this excuse when he appealed: "I was the third guy to hit in my group, and I had just as much right to the same wind that the first two guys had."

At the 2004 Honda Classic a new course debuted and featured thought-provoking green complexes created by antistrategist Tom Fazio. Jay Delsing opened the third round as a single. He never had to wait and took a mind-boggling 3 hours, 23 minutes to complete a round by himself. The rest of the field played in twosomes and took more than 4½ hours to finish eighteen holes.

The recent surge in driving distances has made most par 5s reachable, and now, many short par 4s driveable by everyone on the PGA Tour.

AND COMING SOON TO A COURSE NEAR YOU . . .

Few course owners can relate to Cog Hill owner and operator Frank Jemsek's slow-play–related revenue decline. In the busy summer months his courses are getting less play. Not because golfers have lost interest in the Lemont, Illinois, facility, but because so many players now wait for certain greens to clear.

Armed with hot balls and drivers, many are now able to drive the green on a short par 4 or get home in two on a par 5. Or they believe a potential miracle shot should make them wait.

Tee times thus need more spacing. And with Cog Hill rounds taking longer and only so much sunlight, some customers are either turned away while others are forced to play less than eighteen holes.

Not only does waiting lead to fewer rounds on busy days, but also golfers are leaving the course less satisfied. Some don't show up if they can't get in eighteen.

This waiting problem isn't relegated to Cog Hill. It's already happening across the land.

Players have to wait for the green to clear on par 4s as they would par 3s. Meaning, logjams where there once never were logjams!

The overall effect of the tepid play is brutal. Crowds are bored, players look numb, and perhaps it's not a surprise that attendance is flat everywhere you look outside Phoenix and the majors.

In contrast, John Daly, Luke Donald, and Chris Riley provided a glimpse into the world of fast play during the 2004 Buick Invitational sudden-death playoff. They pulled their clubs and played. No pacing, no twitching, no backing off, no painful pre-shot routine, and most of all, no waiting.

Faced with declining 2004 television ratings, PGA Tour commissioner Tim Finchem was asked by *Golfweek* to name his favorite moment of the "West Coast Swing."

Finchem instead pointed out what was not his no. 1 moment: "I picked on Chris Riley about this. If he makes the putt at eighteen in San Diego [in his playoff against John Daly at the Buick Invitational], we go into the *60 Minutes* time frame, our rating goes up probably a full point. Chris crushed me."

Sliding into the *60 Minutes* time slot may help the PGA Tour convince networks that their "product" is healthy. But a full point ratings bump won't help the rest of golf. Nor will incidents like the slow-play disaster that took place during the 2004 Buick Classic.

Newsday's Greg Logan wrote, "Judging by the backup on every tee on the front nine yesterday, it could have been a typical Saturday at Bethpage State Park, where anything under a 6-hour round is considered quick. But it was the third round of the Buick Classic at ritzy Westchester Country Club."

PGA Tour official Slugger White said it's normal now for players to reach Westchester's 565-yard fifth hole in two shots, as well as the 505-yard ninth. He told reporters that in the past, maybe 20 percent of the field could drive the par-4 tenth, and then White declared, "We've probably got 90 percent of them driving it."

Then Slugger White dropped this bombshell, almost assuredly receiving a small bank account withdrawal from commissioner Tim Finchem's Office-of-Fines-for-Saying-What's-Really-on-Your-Mind: "In all my years out here, I haven't seen anything like today. We've got a situation now where I really feel like the ball is going too far. We've got guys driving the ball farther than they ever have."

Vijay Singh said of the Westchester Saturday slow-play fiasco: "The golf course is too short. We're hitting the ball so much farther with the dryer conditions. We've got to have no. 10 and no. 7 as call-up holes. When you don't do that, that's where the backup comes . . . it's not waiting for 5 minutes. It's waiting for 15, 20, 25 minutes at some holes, and that's not the way to play golf."

Fred Couples brusquely walked past reporters and also turned down a request to be interviewed. Then he turned around and said, "Let me put it this way: I wouldn't have come out and watched today. You might as well have stayed home. It took two players 5 hours to play? On this course?"

As long as technology goes unregulated, slow-play problems will keep surfacing.

TO BIFURCATE OR
NOT TO BIFURCATE

THE PGA TOUR PONDERS THE RAMIFICATIONS OF MAKING ITS OWN EQUIPMENT RULES

"My feeling is that the USGA and the R&A someday are going to have to sepa-rate the amateur player and the professional. They do that in other sports like baseball. Sammy Sosa and Mark McGuire, they play in these great stadiums, but if they had aluminum bats every stadium would be obsolete."

—PETE DYE

NASCAR puts restrictor plates on its stock cars and Major League Baseball requires wood bats. Such modifications are created to main-tain the entertainment value, safety, and integrity of these professional sports.

The PGA Tour has traditionally relied on the USGA to make equipment rules that have little to do with maintaining the tour's entertainment value (nor should they). But the widening gap between the recreational game and PGA Tour play has caused observers to urge the tour to create its own golf ball restrictions to keep the sport entertaining through play that the average fan can relate to.

"The jump in the golf ball this year is ridiculous," said Jack Nicklaus in early 2003. Nicklaus has advocated a competition ball with flight-limiting specifications for 20 years. "Look at the statistics per average player. It's something like 11 [more] yards per player. You take 11 yards and add that to eighteen holes, it's almost 200 yards. I think every golf course that was [lengthened] in 2002 is already obsolete."

As an architect, Nicklaus is concerned with the effect of the longer ball.

"I'm playing roughly the same clubs, and maybe less, into a green that I did in my prime," Nicklaus said. "If I'm doing that, what are guys like Ernie Els and Tiger [Woods] doing? . . . There's only one thing to do and that's to change the golf ball. Get control of the golf ball."

Nick Faldo, winner of six majors, blames the USGA and the Royal and Ancient Golf Club of St. Andrews. "The R&A and the USGA have just blown it," he said. "The horse has bolted so far past the gate that it's in stud."

Paul McGinley, the 2002 European Ryder Cup hero from Ireland, compares the emerging emphasis on high-tech equipment to the build-the-best-car philosophy that has undermined the once hugely popular Formula One racing.

"They've got to find a way to slow the ball down," McGinley said. "They have to sit up and realize that this is getting to be a problem and if they don't, we're going to fall into the same trap as Formula One, and that has me worried."

A "tournament ball" was suggested as early as 1927, when Bobby Jones believed such a distance cap would let architects construct character-rich golf courses in the 6,300-yard range. He feared a wave of 7,000-yard "championship" courses that would take too long to play and overemphasize distance. Talk of equipment regulation has surfaced intermittently through the years, but never has a restricted ball been more frequently advocated than now.

"I am not totally against technology, but they do have to put a governor on the golf ball," Els said recently after his fifth victory in six starts, during which he scored a total of 100 strokes under par.

In 2002, Els averaged 281.4 yards a drive in the United States. After changing to the new Titleist driver and Pro V1x ball, his average rose to 303.3 yards in 2003 PGA Tour events.

At the Phoenix Open in January 2003, forty players averaged more than 300 yards for the week. Only John Daly finished the 2002 U.S. season with an average driving distance of 300-plus yards. Nine players did it in 2003, and the top twenty all averaged more than 297 yards per drive.

One of pro golf's longtime selling points has been that everyday players use the same rules and equipment as the tour professional. The PGA Tour emphasizes this connection because such a bond encourages regular golfers to follow the weekly professional events. The golf equipment industry centers its marketing campaigns around tour players because of the parallels between recreational and pro golf.

Sensing a growing separation between professional and recreation golf and thus a potential long-term threat to viewer interest, PGA Tour commissioner Tim Finchem has hinted that golf needs to re-examine the shift toward the kind of one-dimensional power game that has made professional tennis so much less interesting to watch.

Still, Finchem remained emphatic that he wants no part of equipment rule making.

"There are lots of reasons we should not be in that business," he said in early 2003. "If at some point it appears that they're not going to come to pass, we would have to reevaluate whether we ought to become involved in equipment rule making."

Two weeks and a 376-yard Els drive later, Finchem seemed less opposed to the idea of creating different equipment rules for professionals.

"We are anxious because we are continuing to see some distance enhancements in a short period of time," Finchem told the *Palm Beach Post*. "Unless something happens, we may have to move toward a system of bifurcating the equipment specs for amateurs and professionals."

Galleries are undoubtedly thrilled by long drives. But Finchem believes that television viewers will be unable to relate to drives like Phil Mickelson's recent tee shot that reached the green on the TPC Scottsdale's 403-yard par-4 tenth hole. Creative approach play, short-game wizardry, and heroic recovery shots translate better to television, the PGA Tour's $850-million partner.

"There is some point—nobody knows where it is—when the amateur player feels divorced and doesn't really appreciate the game at this level, just because it's so different that it doesn't become particularly relevant,"

Finchem said. "The second thing is, if everybody is driving every par 4, it's not particularly interesting to watch."

The USGA has long insisted that one set of rules for all is the essence of golf and any departure would be bad for the sport. The organization then posted an online interview in early 2003 with executive director David Fay in which he hinted that "bifurcation" might be an option.

"I believe a burning issue facing the game is whether the talent gap between the best players in the world and the rest of us is widening to the point where we need to consider a more restrictive set of equipment rules for the most highly skilled players," Fay said.

A few months later at the U.S. Open in June, Olympia Fields's ninth (496 yards) and eighteenth (460 yards) holes saw sand wedge second-shot approaches. Fay insisted that he was "comfortable" with the distance situation, but that any further increases might require USGA action.

Finchem will struggle to sell a golf ball rollback to players who don't want to upset their endorsement deals or hit shorter drives for the long-term good of the game. However, except for a handful of top stars, successful players earn far more in PGA Tour prize money than from equipment company endorsement deals, meaning the tour will ultimately get its way.

"You're seeing an evolution occurring and I don't know if you can change the evolution of the game," says Olin Browne, a player and member of the PGA Tour policy board. He does not see a tournament ball on the horizon but concedes that the issue needs to be watched.

If ratings continue to decline or fans defect as professional play becomes less interesting, the PGA Tour may leave the sidelines and enter the ball-regulation business.

PART IV

THE USGA:

Asleep at the Wheel

"There has been a critical failure of leadership. There are many intelligent people who don't understand where the USGA stands."

—Grant Spaeth, former USGA president (1991–92)

Here's what the USGA does well.

The USGA Green Section's Turf Advisory Service, composed of eighteen agronomists, visits about 10 percent of the 16,000 golf facilities in the United States for a fee and at the invitation of the course. They tour the courses with local officials and offer solutions to various golf course maintenance problems.

Most of the green section experts preach maintenance values that call for less water, fewer chemicals, and other ways to create better playing conditions without excessive expense or negative environmental impact. The USGA is also one of the true innovators and leaders in turf grass research. This department alone makes the USGA valuable to golf's future. In 2002, it handed out $1.45 million in grants to fund turf grass research at thirty-four universities.

The USGA Foundation is a relatively new grant-giving unit that appears to be improving the sport by supporting ways that make golf more affordable and accessible. Thanks to a bit of good fortune, some of the more creative past USGA committee members have been involved in its creation, so the USGA Foundation may be more than just a feel-good, vanity-driven offshoot of the USGA.

One of the more interesting foundation projects is a partnership with the National Golf Course Owners Association called "Kids on the Course," where juniors in participating USGA–sanctioned programs are offered $1 green fees at participating courses during their off-peak times.

The USGA has also generously donated money, computers, equipment, and lightning detectors to state and regional golf associations that could not afford such technology.

The USGA's museum and library staff is also first rate and looks for ways to improve exhibits and care for artifacts despite limited resources. The staff focuses on preservation, but have a difficult time getting the money they need to protect their books, memorabilia, and periodicals. Key components of the USGA's collection are said to be deteriorating. There is a dire need for improved storage space, but little is on the drawing board to address the issue. If you have a chance to visit the USGA museum in New Jersey, go.

The USGA has thousands of volunteers who travel to tournaments and serve as rules officials. These are quality folks doing a tough, time-consuming job, sometimes at their own expense. They do it out of a love for the sport and a respect for the rules.

Now that you are aware of their course setup boondoggles and failure to foresee the symptoms from shelving their "optimization" test, it's important to understand what has distracted the USGA from doing a better job of making friends and accumulating capital.

". . . the USGA acts like a body that prefers to be loved, understood and above all, rich."

—Frank Hannigan, former USGA
executive director (1983–89)

The self-proclaimed "legal guardian" of the sport is now armed with in-house lawyers that reportedly are consulted very seldom. The organization prefers to take most of its legal advice from expensive outside law firms who have, by all accounts, served them very well. Mixed in are the "legal" opinions of past presidents and executive committee members, a majority of whom are attorneys.

With all of those lawyers looking out for the best interests of the USGA and golf, some might ask how the organization has allowed the sport to become essentially deregulated, a situation that severely undermines its position as a regulatory body.

The answer is simple. Compromises. Some subtle, some blatant, and some that are just plain inexplicable.

Consider the USGA's healthy television contract with NBC. In the final year of the previous ABC deal, the USGA received $12.785 million from television networks ($7 million from ABC). In 2003, NBC and other international broadcasters paid just over $49.31 million to televise the various USGA events.

The new income feeds the swelling operating budget, which came in at $115 million for 2003, nearly three times what it was 10 years ago. (The 1994 annual report listed $44.4 million in expenses to run the USGA.)

With their millions, NBC has purchased an unusually cooperative atmosphere, as pointed out by John Feinstein in his bestseller *Open*. (The book draws ire from some USGA staffers because of Feinstein's unprecedented access to the executive director and several sensitive meetings.)

From Feinstein we learn that NBC has the power to influence and even shuffle player tee times if they wish. The USGA selects tournament hole locations based on NBC camera locations. Tee times for the entire field are juggled so the tournament will end as late as possible to provide NBC with a nice Sunday evening prime-time lead-in and the best possible Nielson rating. This practice nearly proved disastrous in 2002 at Bethpage when a rain delay forced Tiger to finish off his win in the dark.

"The people we looked to in order to maintain the integrity of the game failed us. They didn't have enough foresight or courage. I lay total blame at the foot of the USGA."
—DEANE BEMAN, FORMER COMMISSIONER OF THE PGA TOUR

Who runs the USGA?

The current executive director is David Fay, who reports to a fifteen-member executive committee. The USGA staff is based in Far Hills, New Jersey. They report to Fay, who then works with, steers, and ultimately has to explain and justify what the volunteer executive committee decides to do "for the good of the game."

The USGA regional staff members, president, and immediate past presidents oversee the selection of volunteers for various subcommittees that traditionally feed the fifteen-member board its constituents. More recently, fewer executive committee members have been coming from the subcommittees, which may explain the apparent inability to grasp fundamental problems when it comes time to debate and decide issues presented to the executive committee. Personal connections or ties to U.S. Open sites in the current rotation seem to be the way many future executive committee members will be selected.

The executive committee's handling of amateur status, *Golf Journal*, the dwindling membership program, and the Russian Tea Room purchase illustrate how the group has lost sight of its mission.

WHAT AMATEUR STATUS?

". . . an amateur golfer, with golf skill and reputation, can accept free or discounted equipment from a manufacturer or distributor of such equipment. The above changes have been well received by golfers in the U.S."

—*2002 USGA* ANNUAL REPORT

Did you notice that amateur prodigy Michelle Wie wore a hat emblazed with Titleist and FootJoy logos in her many 2003 tournament appearances? Her hats also happen to color-coordinate with her outfits.

It wasn't long ago that someone at the USGA might have thought it unseemly for an *amateur* golfer to wear a choreographed company hat or shirt every day at a major amateur event. And not long ago they would have required the player to change into an anonymous shirt or cover the logos. It happened to me in a local USGA qualifier. When I was a collegiate golfer in the early '90s, I actually had to put tape over the college logo on my hat! But that was when amateur status still meant something and the USGA thankfully went overboard at times trying to protect it.

Back in those halcyon days, USGA officials might have balked if Wie had announced to the press that she planned to make a round of visits to the manufacturers' test ranges in Carlsbad on her way back home to Hawaii. Now such a visit is just a day in the life of a high-profile amateur.

And a few might have winced if Wie had appeared in a *People* ad, a publication that is owned by Time-Warner, which also owns *Sports Illustrated*, *Golf Magazine*, *TNT*, etc.

Nor would the old USGA have been comfortable if Wie had trained at the International Management Group (IMG)–owned golf academy in Florida. (IMG is an enormous agency that represents professional athletes, runs tournaments, negotiates sponsorship deals, and, wait, that's everything related to running professional golf!)

The old USGA might have questioned whether such activities placed Wie outside of compliance with the principles governing amateur status. The new USGA has accepted the same kind of compromises to professionalism as those made by the International Olympic Committee. But sleep easier, the USGA still goes after the *real* outlaws of amateur golf— like Mike Freeman of Orlando.

Freeman is a scratch golfer who arrived one day at a Florida course for his regular game. It just happened to be the day Tiger Woods and Buick were filming those clever ads where Tiger pops out of the uh, woods, and challenges an unsuspecting foursome to a spontaneous closest-to-the-pin competition as hidden cameras catch the looks on surprised faces.

When Mike Freeman hit a shot closer to the pin than Woods, he was given the keys to a Buick and earned a spot in a television ad. The event was unplanned and unrehearsed. Freeman had no idea he was being filmed or that a car really awaited if he outplayed Woods.

Guess what? Freeman lost his amateur status for a year and a half. The defending Orlando City Amateur Champion, Freeman was not allowed to defend his title. He had to petition the USGA because the free-car-for-a-hole-in-one award is a violation of the rules, and yes, it's nice that the USGA still enforces one aspect of amateur status. But the length of his punishment and the fact that they even bothered to suspend Freeman's status appears inconsistent when his appearance in the ad was key to his status change. None of his playing partners who appeared in the ad or any other golfers featured by Buick lost their status.

In light of compromises made for Wie or for former professional players who have become reinstated amateurs, the Freeman situation looks even sillier.

Dillard Pruitt won a PGA Tour event and thousands of dollars over a 10-year career. A reinstated amateur, he now works for the PGA Tour as a rules official and by all accounts is a great guy. But, because he works for the tour, he probably pays for a round of golf about as often as he did when he was a PGA Tour member—that is, never.

Pruitt had to sit out 3 years to regain his amateur status, which he was granted despite his continued ties to professional golf and the perks that go with it. Why should Pruitt be allowed to regain his amateur status at all? Amazingly, if Pruitt decides to turn pro again, he can still decide to reapply once more for amateur status!

Why does the USGA allow amateurs to accept free equipment that can be construed as an endorsement, while all Mike Freeman did was spontaneously accept a gift without endorsing Buick? And Freeman was considered a professional while Pruitt and Wie are amateurs in good standing?

Then there is Nick Flanagan, 2003 U.S. Amateur champion. Here's a young man who came from Australia with the financial backing of a local foundation similar to many other nonprofit organizations internationally. He needed aid because his dad is a low-wage coal miner. He accepted the same assistance package that many other fine young Australian golfers have been receiving for years, including travel expenses, free food, and lodging here in the United States.

Flanagan's opponent in the U.S. Amateur final, Casey Wittenburg, had attended the IMG–owned David Leadbetter Academy for 4 years. The Leadbetter Academy charges an annual five-digit tuition fee. (Though some scholarships are also offered by IMG.) Either way, once the student is in the door, there are perks even a professional golfer would love. For example, academy teachers can fly in and caddy for you at amateur events without violating any amateur status rules. Titleist is a sponsor of the school, so surely no one tees it up without the proper (free) equipment.

But Nick Flanagan made a mistake that prompted an investigation: He won the 2003 U.S. Amateur. Flanagan was investigated for accepting expense money, something other Aussie's have done before him. Then he had to go and mess it all up by winning! Well, he didn't lose his title, the USGA was merely going through the motions and he was cleared of wrongdoing, but the investigation both at home and by the USGA tainted his unlikely win.

Here's another troubling sign that the USGA allows consumerism to trump amateurism. For years, companies have been allowed to do ball and equipment surveys at the U.S. Amateur and U.S. Junior Amateurs. Some folks in the old USGA might have said it wasn't wholesome to allow a survey representative on the first tee to ask 16-year-old boys and girls what clubs and balls they're playing and then allow the companies to advertise the survey results the following week.

Since companies have been known to give their products to young golfers in hopes of creating "brand loyalty" if and when it comes time for the newly minted young professionals to sign on the endorsement deal–dotted line, the survey lets the companies know who is and who is not using their equipment. (We know they can figure it out anyway at American Junior Golf Association [AJGA] events, and they should have to do it somewhere besides a USGA event.)

The USGA rules state, "an amateur golfer may accept equipment from anyone dealing in such equipment provided no advertising is involved." Yet the USGA is failing to protect the spirit of its own amateur status rules by allowing the survey groups to tabulate and then share those results for marketing purposes.

Also consider the inequity of what could potentially be going on behind locker room doors. Certain amateurs may be getting more freebies because they could be PGA Tour players some day, while others with limited long-term marketing appeal stand to get fewer freebies, if any. And a golfer at the University of Florida is going to have more access to free equipment than say, a player from Cal State Dominguez Hills.

The USGA's David Fay suggests that the marketplace will work itself in this instance as well. He's right, some people will just get better treatment than others, but not always because they are better players.

A similar compromise to professionalism was a disaster for tennis and ultimately undermined the stature and credibility of the U.S. Tennis Association (USTA).

Why has the USGA failed to learn from the mistakes of the USTA? Perhaps because they didn't read up on their history before they joined the USGA. Or maybe they just don't listen to past members. Either way, thanks to the elimination of *Golf Journal*, they have one less place to read about issues in golf.

MICHELLE WIE'S STRUGGLE WITH
AMATEUR STATUS CONTINUES

*"As long as Michelle Wie remains an amateur there will be specu-
lation about her educational future. Mighty Stanford . . . is said
to be the front-runner for her prowess. Should it ever come down
to IMG vs Stanford, I'll take IMG and give the points."*
—FRANK HANNIGAN

When Michelle Wie nearly made the cut at 2004's Sony Open,
her Titleist hats included another logo for the Leadbetter Golf
Academy and a pair of flags representing the USGA and state
of Hawaii.

The rules says it's OK for an amateur to wear items with corporate logos as long as they are readily available to the public.
Since no one can purchase a Titleist cap with a Hawaiian flag
and a plug for the Leadbetter Academy, the USGA's David Fay
had to fly halfway across the world to lecture Wie on violating
the amateur status rules.

No more color-coordinated Titleist hats for you, young lady.
But say, have you got plans for July?

Yes, as a reward for misbehaving, Fay admitted to fighting
for and securing Wie an invitation to the U.S. Women's Open.
This certainly didn't upset any of the executives at NBC, where
Fay has developed an unusually close relationship.

Of course Wie deserved to be playing in the Open based on
her win in the U.S. Women's Amateur Public Links and her top-
five finish at the season's first major, but the timing could not
have been worse for those hoping to see amateur status rules
remain relevant.

Wie's family regularly calls the USGA to check on violations,
while they flirt with every manufacturer known to man, setting
themselves up for the best possible payday when Michelle turns
pro. In July 2004, Darrell Rover reported on *ESPN.com*:

Michelle Wie is playing her cards just right. Shirt, shoes, and socks by Adidas. Glove by FootJoy. A cap emblazoned with "Leadbetter Golf," the golf school in Florida where she honed her swing last winter. And in her bag . . . "I have a Nike driver, I have Titleist irons, Scotty Cameron putter [Titleist], Vokey wedges [Titleist], and a Titleist Pro V1X [ball]," Wie said, rattling off name after name of potential products that one day soon could be vying for her endorsement, after finishing even-par 71 through Thursday's first round of the Women's U.S. Open.

The backstage soap opera grew more interesting when it was revealed that Wie's first instructor, Gary Gilchrist, had left the David Leadbetter Academy and joined up with a Nike staffer to possibly lure Wie away from her inevitable destination: a life of lucrative endorsements and playing around the world at the behest of IMG.

Remember, according to the rules, an amateur golfer "must not take any action for the purpose of becoming a professional golfer." An "action" in that scenario would include "directly or indirectly receiving services or payment from a professional agent or sponsor, commercial or otherwise."

So you're probably asking, how is it that IMG, a big agency, can own a golf school for aspiring amateur golfers while the students retain their amateur status? Good question.

The behind-the-ropes struggle to capitalize on Wie's success was finally resolved according to the Golf Channel's Brian Hewitt, who wrote that the Wie family had selected teacher David Leadbetter over Gary Gilchrist and that Nike "has assigned Greg Nared to spend time with the Wie family and develop a relationship."

"We get along very well," B. J. Wie said of the Nike relationship. "But we don't talk about business. If Michelle needs a club, Greg can provide the product."

Ah, the purity of modern-day amateur golf!

GOLF JOURNAL, R.I.P.

"As a result of a growing USGA membership, Golf Journal *reaches an ever-wider audience."*

—*2002 USGA* ANNUAL REPORT

If you find the inconsistencies in enforcing amateur status troubling, consider the USGA executive committee's decision to halt publication of *Golf Journal*.

A USGA tradition for almost 55 years, the magazine was the primary reason many golfers joined or retained their USGA membership. Claiming that it cost more than $4 million a year to publish, the USGA dropped the publication in early 2003 in favor of a newsletter, the prototype of which was created by executive committee member Craig Ammerman's former company. Members now receive a year-end annual whose prototype was envisioned by subcommittee member and former *Sports Illustrated* managing editor Mark Mulvoy.

The first edition of the "Inside the USGA" newsletter was so plain, one golfer wrote on an Internet discussion group that the quality of his church newsletter was higher. The year-end annual was attractively produced, though tainted by the inclusion of advertising that *Golf Journal* never had.

Since dropping *Golf Journal* in early 2003, USGA sources say the organization has lost more than 20 percent of its total membership as of October 2003, with many more not renewing their memberships when the big year-end renewal kicked in. The main reason for these folks leaving is the departure of *Golf Journal*, again, according to insiders who'd like to remain anonymous (and keep their jobs).

Former USGA President Reg Murphy, who strongly favored dropping *Golf Journal*, insisted that only twenty-five people called to cancel their memberships in protest. (Several other past presidents and staff members were horrified at the news, and the 20 percent or more membership decline is widely cited within the USGA's gossipy inner circle.)

USGA director of communications Marty Parkes counters that there has only been a 9 percent membership drop from October 2002 to October 2003. Furthermore, he says USGA research shows that "no longer receiving" *Golf Journal* placed fourteenth out of fifteenth on a list of reasons people cited for dropping their memberships. The weak economy and the depressed state of golf were more likely reasons for the significant 9 percent drop, according to Parkes.

(That there were actually fifteen potential reasons for quitting the membership program is amazing in itself!)

So for a moment let's give the USGA a break and say *Golf Journal* was *not* a big reason 70,000 people chose to keep their $15 in 2003. The organization has shelved a valuable source for communicating the USGA message (if there is a coherent message besides "legal guardians of the game"). However, part of the *Golf Journal* elimination equation was to include an increased Web presence that has not been detected, as *usga.org* is thin on content and the replacement newsletter includes stories written by an executive committee member instead of professional writers.

"Golf has a rich tradition in the essay form, as do baseball, boxing, and fishing. But it's hard to find articles that demand more of the reader—a few hours and careful concentration and consideration. The U.S. Golf Association recently dropped Golf Journal. *Its articles weren't essays, but the editors at least encouraged writers to probe areas and write articles about subjects other than tour golf and golfers."*

—LORNE RUBENSTEIN, AUTHOR AND COLUMNIST

Golf journalism lost a source for stories that other golf magazines wouldn't feel compelled to cover. Some of those stories were perhaps too off-beat—truck-driving golfers, for example. And yes, tournament stories 2 months after the event are not particularly exciting except to the participants, their families, and host sites. On the other hand, they provided details that again would not be documented in the major magazines or newspapers—details that later prove crucial to historians.

Other *Golf Journal* stories, in hindsight, provided the kind of forward-thinking journalism that golf lacks today, such as articles on land and water usage or Frank Hannigan's 1974 *Golf Journal* biographic essay on A. W. Tillinghast that sparked today's widespread recognition of classic architecture.

Golf Journal mattered, and it could have continued as a valuable tool for presenting the USGA's case on issues of interest to avid golfers who desperately want to support the organization.

You don't throw the baby out with the bathwater. The USGA should have revamped the content if they felt the magazine wasn't working.

Judging by the current executive committee conflicts of interest and refusal to admit mistakes, *Golf Journal* won't be coming back any time soon no matter how many members the USGA loses.

DWINDLING MEMBERSHIP

"The USGA—which already has over $160 million in cash in the bank, for what purpose, God knows!—seems determined to give Major League Baseball a run for the fans' money in the greed, avarice and vulgarity department . . . when it comes to prostrating itself before the corporate fatcat patronage, the USGA also seems set on proving itself without peer."

—MICHAEL THOMAS, *GOLF DIGEST* CONTRIBUTING EDITOR

We don't need no stinking members!

That seems to be the executive committee's attitude. After all, they have television contracts. And they can erect a few more U.S. Open corporate tents if need be.

One *very* famous old venue in line to host the Open on a *very* special anniversary has been told they need to find more than fifty corporate tent sites if they want to host the Open again.

No move has been more suspect than the USGA's recent decision to move U.S. Open corporate tents from low-profile off-course locations to the heart of the action. It's all part of doing business in the marketplace of professional golf.

So what if having fewer USGA members means they have to erect more tents between say, the sixth and fourteenth holes at Pebble Beach? Big deal. And who cares if Tiger Woods has to back off of a shot when intoxicated "corporate partners" disrupt the national championship? Those good inebriated folks are paying the bills! They certainly spend much more than those who respectfully sent in a measly $15–$25 and expected a nice magazine in return.

But, maybe those membership dollars were more valuable than the USGA thought. Let's now assume *Golf Journal* was the most important and cherished benefit for members and cost almost $6 per member per year to produce. (That's assuming a 2002 year-end membership total of more than 700,000 and *Golf Journal*'s reported, though mysteriously bloated, $4.05 million budget.)

With a presumed 20 percent membership drop (150,000 × $15 = $2.25 million), that annual $6 per member suddenly looks more affordable. And no matter what market research the USGA says it can point to, *Golf Journal* was a more tangible benefit for USGA members than a bag tag.

Why else is the membership program important? Let's start with the idea that at its peak, it brought in upwards of $25 million, no small amount for an organization looking to not rely so heavily on U.S. Open revenues. But by dropping *Golf Journal* and shrugging off the membership program in favor of other revenue streams that may or may not pan out, the executive committee seems to be saying, "If the people who support golf do not like what we're doing, they can just keep their money."

And that's what it appears the golfers are doing, in droves.

One obvious benefit of not having an official magazine is that you don't have to put your positions in print. The negative is obvious, though. No longer is there a classy stage from which to state your case to the people who buy the equipment, pay the green fees, join the clubs, maintain handicaps, and make the USGA relevant.

If *Golf Journal* was the primary benefit for many who join the USGA membership program, which not long ago had a base of 1 million members, how could the USGA jeopardize that program? After all, having a healthy membership totally reinforces the notion that you have the support of devoted golfers when manufacturers are trying to weaken your cause of protecting the sport.

Perhaps the cause isn't nearly as organized as one would hope.

THE RUSSIAN TEA ROOM DEBACLE

"I needed a half million dollars to buy a script. Blockbuster, but quality. No mutants or maniacs. This is going to be my Driving Miss Daisy.*"*

—HORROR FILM PRODUCER HARRY ZIMM IN *GET SHORTY*

Turning New York City's Russian Tea Room restaurant into a USGA museum would be former executive committee secretary Eric Gleacher's *Driving Miss Daisy*. Instead, it is another sign of how distracted and self-serving the USGA executive committee has become.

According to former USGA President Reed MacKenzie, the bluecoats wished to restore "a prominent presence in the city" where the USGA had been headquartered prior to their 1972 move to Far Hills, New Jersey.

By creating a high-tech golf center in New York City, the USGA promised "to attract a large and diverse audience, with engaging interactive and multimedia exhibits" while encouraging "the development of active educational and outreach programs." However, it was *not* going to be a much-needed storage place for withering artifacts, nor a true museum because there were no plans to significantly expand displays of memorabilia.

Ego and diversification of revenue streams, not outreach, were the primary objectives here, according to several sources.

On November 18, 2002, the USGA announced that it had purchased the bankrupt Russian Tea Room restaurant and building for $16 million. They got a really big kitchen complete with all the old forks and plates. The Picasso reproductions adorning the walls were thrown in, too.

The purchase was the work of then USGA secretary and de facto in-house acquisitions man, venture capitalist Eric Gleacher. How, you ask, does one man push through such a big-ticket item when he is on a committee with fourteen others, supported by an even larger paid staff to research such projects?

A fine golfer and former marine, Gleacher began his Wall Street career in 1968 as an associate at Lehman Brothers. In January 1990 he founded his own investment bank, Gleacher & Co., which specialized in complicated mergers. He later merged his firm with NatWest, a leading U.K. global bank, but later repurchased the company from NatWest.

Gleacher contributed $15 million to the University of Chicago Business School to help finance a new building in downtown Chicago, and he donated $6.1 million to Northwestern University to construct an indoor golf practice facility for varsity golfers while endowing the men's and women's golf team budgets in perpetuity.

Not a bad resume! And obviously a generous fellow.

Since joining the USGA executive committee in 1996, Gleacher has reorganized the USGA's finances and invested in a few higher-risk funds including, ironically, technology funds. Gleacher urged the organization to diversify its revenue streams so that it didn't rely so heavily on the U.S. Open profits (currently $9 out of every $10 the USGA earns). And he structured a financial plan to guide the USGA after his departure from the executive committee.

In the late 1990s when the tech boom and NASDAQ were skyrocketing at an astonishing rate, Gleacher presented the executive committee with a glimpse into a future that painted a rosy financial picture, one so flush with capital that the USGA would have to diversify its interests to spend all of the money it would make, just to avoid the problems that go with being a "nonprofit" organization. And how could his fellow committee members *not* listen to him? After all, the portfolio had peaked at a value of at least $200 million before the tech bubble burst.

Gleacher had fellow executive committee members convinced that all would be well with USGA finances. His investments and other revenue streams would bring in so much money, which combined with U.S. Open profits, might swell the USGA war chest. A total of as much as $300 million was cited by several sources as a prediction heard during the height of the technology stock boom.

Meanwhile, most of us on the outside looking in assumed the financial buildup was designed to scare off hawkish manufacturers. It stood to reason that a wealthy USGA would be ready to go to court if the companies chose to duke it out there, and thus, a worst-case scenario $50-million defeat in court wouldn't harm the USGA.

Instead, that notion appears to have been a minor part of the equation, if a consideration at all. As a member of the museum committee, Gleacher believed that creating a new USGA museum in New York City would not only help the USGA spend some of its excess capital, but also would create a new revenue stream that would take some of the pressure off of the U.S. Open to produce each year.

Yes, that's right, the new museum was supposed to make money. Lots of money—in theory, anyway.

In the early 1990s the USGA flirted with possible museum sites in Atlanta and the Monterey Peninsula. The New York City idea resurfaced because certain USGAers believed the lack of a Big Apple presence was hurting their stature in dealing with city-based companies. (Meanwhile, amateur golfing great and former executive committee member Carole Semple Thompson lobbied for upgrading Golf House to get it in compliance with the "Americans with Disabilities Act" before venturing east of Far Hills.)

After a search, Gleacher settled on the bankrupt Russian Tea Room restaurant as the best site for a museum. This new USGA city location would accept admission fees for the 1,000 visitors expected daily. (USGA fantasy: 300,000 visitors a year at say, $10 a piece—that's $3 million a year!) The USGA would also generate revenue from a museum conference center where Wall Street big shots could iron out the details of their next white-collar crimes, all the while surrounded by portraits of Bobby Jones and Old Tom Morris. Shoot, they probably even envisioned golf nuts getting married there.

The much-needed city presence would apparently grow the game by leaps and bounds, but the deal had to be finalized quickly and quietly to get the museum up and running in time for the 2004 U.S. Open at Shinnecock Hills. After all, they had to have some place to host early week cocktail parties!

The $16 million Russian Tea Room purchase was approved by the executive committee with the understanding that the cost to renovate its six floors into the Gleacher–USGA Museum and Banquet Hall would cost in the neighborhood of $15 million.

But after buying the building, the USGA received estimates from the prominent ESI Design firm that suddenly rocketed to $40 million just to make the building habitable. That's $25 million more than pre-approved figures. So the USGA executive committee wisely decided to get out.

Before the deal collapsed, the USGA cooperated for a lengthy *New Yorker* piece written by the celebrated John McPhee. The March 31, 2003, article was loaded with anecdotes referring to the organization as a progressive bastion of multiculturalism in the otherwise elitist world of golf. We learned that the USGA has been a friend to the common man, the Native American, and the public golfer. *(It should be noted that two African Americans and four women have served on the USGA executive committee in its 110-year history.)*

The *New Yorker* article lacked any insights from either executive director David Fay or Gleacher. Instead, staff member and curator Rand Jerris acted as their front man. A wise decision in hindsight, as he is now in charge of answering questions about a fiasco that wasn't his doing.

In announcing the decision *not* to convert the space into a museum and to put the building back on the market, the USGA suggested they were troubled by a New York State law that contained "unique provisions that provide for oversight of museums by the state's Board of Regents." The provisions mandated the creation of a board of trustees who "could potentially limit the USGA's ability to control the facility and its collections."

Shouldn't at least one of their many lawyers have alerted them to this law before the USGA bought the Russian Tea Room? Or perhaps the executive director should have seen this problem coming?

No, because the New York Board of Regents was not going to be a problem. Citing the state law was an obvious smokescreen to save face.

The USGA finally unloaded the Tea Room in late 2004, getting $20 million, which was just enough to cover its expenditures on the project (design, taxes, maintenance, real estate commissions). Contrary to what a few remaining USGA supporters claim, this was not a profitable venture.

By now I suspect you are asking, why does the Tea Room mistake matter and what does it have to do with fun, affordability, the technology
debate, and the future of golf?

Plenty.

First, it is another example of the USGA getting distracted from its
mission. The financial black hole to which the organization exposed
itself undermines its credibility even if they wised up in time to cut their
losses. It was also another sign that the executive committee was too
busy developing self-serving projects.

The Tea Room-turned-museum would surely have been a fine place,
with much-needed room for curator Rand Jerris to show off the collection while providing space to store many deteriorating artifacts. (The
current museum does not have a climate-controlled area to preserve its
awesome collection.) However, an expansion of the collection to the new
facility was not part of the plan, undermining any spin that claimed the
city-museum would have been a great source to preserve and show off
golf artifacts.

The Tea Room fiasco also raises questions about Gleacher's plan to
diversify. With dwindling membership income, the USGA is more depen-
dent on U.S. Open revenues to cover its $115 million annual operating
budget.

A downturn in U.S. Open tent or merchandise sales or a sudden change
of heart by television executives could leave the USGA in a less than rosy
financial situation. Taking on a lawsuit from a reckless manufacturer
will be more problematic, meaning decisions will continue to be made to
avoid confrontations with equipment companies eager to bend the rules.
(Translation: Get used to venues like Torrey Pines, where having plenty
of corporate tent space takes priority over course quality.)

Eric Gleacher "retired" from the committee at the end of 2003, ironically the year the Tea Room disaster unfolded. Gleacher confirmed in a
not-so-pretty swan song interview with *Golf World* that "if the USGA is
going to move forward they've got to change the governance."

Some people would argue that they are off to a good start with his
retirement.

PART V

DRIVING UP COST, DRIVING DOWN GOLF:

How Politics, Signatures, Rankings, and Other Pervasive Trends Add Cost and Eliminate Fun

"Pebble Beach really isn't on the ocean. It's on Carmel Bay. Ocean Trails really overlooks the Pacific Ocean. It's the best piece of property I've ever seen."

—DONALD TRUMP, OWNER OF THE NEWLY RENAMED
TRUMP NATIONAL AT LOS ANGELES

"When I bought the course, the bank had $211 million into it. I'm spending $50 million. That must make it the most expensive course on the planet."

—DONALD TRUMP, AGAIN, ON TRUMP NATIONAL L.A.

Besides the back-door deregulation that will do nothing to reduce the expense of golf, other elements tack on cost, time, and aggravation to rounds of golf. Course management companies hide behind double-speak to make it sound like they are appeasing Wall Street expectations or the alleged demands of golfers. This nonsense has combined with politics, rankings, signatures, and an assortment of technology-driven design trends to undermine the values that nurtured golf in the first place. And as the decline in rounds-played proves, this "progress" is not keeping people in the sport.

MBA GOLF

*DOUBLESPEAK AND MODERN BUSINESS MANTRAS
DON'T WORK IN GOLF*

"Bad terminology is the enemy of good thinking."

—WARREN BUFFETT

Warren Buffett is worth a few billion bucks because he tends to stick to common-sense ideals. He recently wrote about big business's latest self-destructive trend: corporate doublespeak.

He was referring to the smoke and mirrors that CEOs and their press release writers send out to cover up their inability to function with integrity. Buffett couched his unusually sarcastic remarks in a golf analogy, mocking today's financial reports: "In golf my score is frequently below par on a pro-forma basis: I have firm plans to restructure my putting stroke and therefore only count the swings I take before reaching the green."

Many consider euphemism-dropping an obnoxious practice. Others, such as skeptical writers, find doublespeak entertaining in its inanity. After all, you have to admire the creativity that allows folks to accept phrases like "working vacation," "preowned cars," and "aggressive tax avoidance."

Golf has reached the point where doublespeak and other MBA practices are no longer funny, most notably in the golf course management business. Corporate speak is now used even by golf's nonprofit governing bodies.

The USGA's David Fay speaks of his "fiduciary responsibility" to the *volunteer* executive committee of his *nonprofit* organization. PGA Tour commissioner Tim Finchem gave his 2002 year-end "state of the tour" press conference and referred to the PGA Tour's "brand," "brands," or "branding," a whopping thirty-six times in 15 minutes. He also couldn't resist dropping "platform" and "franchise," the MBA code words *du jour* that comfort corporate types by subliminally saying, "See, I read *Forbes* too."

As Finchem unveiled the Senior Tour's exciting new name (Champions Tour) and logo (think PGA Tour logo, only with a red swoosh), he declared, "We want to make sure we are well positioned to capitalize on the strength of this brand across our platforms."

Translation: We hope that we can save the Senior Tour by clinging to the popularity Tiger has brought to the regular tour, because we don't know what else to do, so we're getting rid of that dreaded word *senior* and that logo with the old guy in knickers!

Judging by the nonexistent crowds in towns that used to support Senior Tour events, that new logo and name are not working for the, uh, Champions Tour.

According to Hugh Rawson, author of the *Dictionary of Euphemisms and Doublespeak*, the use of suspect terminology reveals "outward and visible signs of our inward anxieties, conflicts, fears, and shames. They are like radioactive isotopes. By tracing them, it is possible to see what has been (and is) going on in our language, our minds, and our culture."

What has been going on in golf is an MBA takeover of the mom-and-pop business side, with, at best, mixed results. These CEO types come armed with an MBA that reinforces their belief in themselves and the management theory mantras that they've been told will work in *any* business environment.

In the golf course management business, many facilities chugged along over the years doing okay on simple business models. Many others were poorly run. Private management companies stepped in and turned around several run-down muni's and often created jobs and better facilities. Great. But then they started becoming publicly traded companies. The execs fantasized about their IPOs and buying second homes in Malibu. We started hearing them repeat Wall Street's favorite mantra, growth. The stock price became everything, a force so great it supersedes logic or sound decision-making.

Enter doublespeak to spin the downward cycle.

Golf management companies should never expect to grow steadily in a business that is cyclical by nature, and worse, often affected by Mother Nature. They tried to grow by paying too much for courses at a time when 3 million people a year were quitting the game. Staggering under massive debt, they skimped on service and maintenance, jumped on the country-club-for-day model that made little long-term sense, and often alienated those who were trying to remain loyal customers.

Now, except for a couple of straight shooters who wisely remain privately held and devoted to customer service, plenty of golf management companies are experiencing growing pains. Instead of telling the truth and trusting people who know golf to help them right the ship, they are dumping bad terminology on us to mask the truth.

The downward cycle started when the language shifted from "public" to "daily fee" courses. Then "marshals" became "player assistants." "Maintenance yards" became "turf care facilities." Now MBA Doublespeak 101 has become downright insulting. A few recent gems:

• We have *"improved the demographics of our customer base."* Aren't all green fees printed on the same paper?

• *"It's a platform to reposition our brand."* Translation: "We're starting over from scratch."

• *"Quality" of rounds is more important to our brand than "quantity."* Fewer rounds played at a higher price is better than a higher number of satisfied repeat customers over the long term? Yep, that's worked really well for all of the "upscale daily fees" who have turned to selling memberships to stay afloat, or the thirty-six-holers that are looking to develop one of their eighteens into town homes.

• *"We are experiencing excess capacity."* The tee sheet's empty, so come on out and tee it up!

• He has left the company *"to spend more time with his family."* A longtime staple of doublespeak, certainly not exclusive to golf. *And come to think of it, he also wants to "pursue other interests"*—hopefully, in the bowling industry.

- *"We can create a unified, focused corporate structure to unlock the full value of our combined property portfolio."* We've gotta merge because the investment bankers say that's the only way to avoid going out of business.

- *"We will not allow this property to be devalued by lowering green fees."* Tell me, how does going broke help your property value? I guess we'll have to ask the bankruptcy judge when he gives away your course for a couple of old gang mowers, a bucket of balls, and a cash payment to be named later.

Many in golf's upper echelon will never understand Warren Buffett's simple advice: Don't invest in a business you fail to understand; buy companies with strong histories of profitability; determine whether management is candid with shareholders; always invest for the long term.

Golf has plenty of talented people. They are capable of making courses profitable and given a little more space to operate, they can turn them into fun places to play over the long haul. But when they have to spend their time trying to get a decision out of the folks who craft the press releases that no one believes, it's pretty hard to get anything done that benefits the customers.

Golf is a sport of integrity. It is also a difficult, expensive pursuit where customers need—ugh, MBAism coming here—"value" to keep coming back, but not the almighty property value or company value that theory-plagued MBAs obsess over.

This is *value*: Give people decent service and a fair green fee on an enjoyable, well-maintained course that can be played in a reasonable amount of time.

Let's hope that straightforward terminology becomes the enemy of bad thinking.

WHY CAN'T THEY BUILD THEM LIKE THEY USED TO?

"Before you build a course with deep bunkers, railroad ties, forced carries and water everywhere, just remember that no Donald Ross course has ever gone Chapter 11."

—LEE TREVINO

Jack Nicklaus was asked to explain the differences between certain golf courses on the Monterey Peninsula's 17-Mile Drive. Nicklaus replied, "Pebble Beach and Cypress Point make you want to play. Spyglass Hill— that's different; that makes you want to go fishing."

His sentiments sum up what many golfers feel when they try to make a distinction between modern designs such as Robert Trent Jones's relentless Spyglass Hill, and gentler, thought-provoking classics like Pebble Beach or Cypress Point. The latter designs bring out the best in us through interesting, intimidating, yet surmountable features. Plenty of modern courses provide a pleasant setting for the game, but few inspire us because there is little thrill in overcoming their difficulties. As Max Behr once said, they are often tests of "will instead of tests of skill."

How distinct is the gap between modern and classic designs? In *Golf Magazine*'s most recent ranking of the top 100 courses in America, just 2 of the first 20 layouts were built after 1940, and both are full-fledged retro-designs inspired by classic architecture.

Golf Digest's list reveals a similar imbalance. Trade publication *Golfweek* has found such a difference between eras that they've split their course ranking into two lists: the top 100 layouts built prior to 1960 and another list of 100 from the modern era.

The discrepancy becomes even more astonishing when you consider that renowned early twentieth–century designers like Alister MacKenzie and George Thomas predicted golf course design would ascend to levels no one in their era could imagine. They thought that future layouts would eventually overshadow the great courses of their day and bring even more players to the game.

Instead, golf has grown in peculiar spurts since the days of MacKenzie and Thomas, with exciting players like Arnold Palmer and Tiger Woods creating great short-term interest, while the lack of fun, affordable, and interesting courses has prevented those euphoric spurts from having a lasting impact.

If you ask modern architects why they can't design courses like Mac-Kenzie did, few acknowledge much of a discrepancy.

"In the so-called 'classic' era, designers picked ideal sites whenever possible where golf holes could be easily fit into interesting terrain," writes Tom Fazio. "But even these ideal sites often had flat or unattractive areas that could be avoided. So designers connected the interesting areas with holes that were not so grand. That's one reason we find a few ordinary holes on some of our more famous courses. Today, we couldn't get away with that."

Some of the modern architects like Fazio sincerely believe that after their designs host a few majors and have time to mature, their work will be considered as good as the "so-called" classics like Shinnecock Hills and Pinehurst, which, according to some architects, thrive on history as much as pure design. These modern architects also point out that the early designers like Donald Ross and A. W. Tillinghast had their choice of great sites and were unrestricted by various bureaucracies and environmental restrictions.

In many cases, today's designers have persuaded the public that they just don't have a chance to create designs of merit or character. Then, how do they explain Sand Hills or Pacific Dunes? These two modern designs incorporate environmentally sensitive site features while joining the top twenty courses in the world.

And how do they explain courses like Riviera and Pine Valley, which at the time of their creation, were considered questionable sites for golf? Or what about places like Oakmont, Oakland Hills, Pinehurst, and Merion, which were by no means spectacular sites? Somehow, they became world-renowned in spite of their land and *before* they hosted multiple major championships.

A small but growing number of traditionalists are spreading the word and explaining why classic courses retain an enduring playing quality. These traditionalists, who preach a "minimalist" design and construction philosophy, build the courses themselves instead of hiring an expensive contractor to interpret their plans. They emphasize two traits that most modern courses lack: naturalness and strategy.

In the 1920s and early 1930s golf architects advocated subtle and natural design features. They placed artistically sculptured bunkers in well-chosen locations so that every shot created options and thus interesting decisions for golfers of all abilities. They were sensitive to the existing terrain. Courses were easily walkable. Few of the master architects like MacKenzie or Ross fought the land, even if it meant they had to include an occasional blind shot. The result for the golfer is a comfortable feeling of playing in natural settings, not over land re-configured and bulldozed for the convenience of carts, subdivisions, or visibility.

Pacific Dunes architect Tom Doak, one of the architects preaching a return to less costly, more natural designs, is devoted to injecting strategy and subtle local knowledge elements into his courses. The idea is to interest all levels of golfers, not just above-average players, and to make the golf interesting and fresh on repeat visits, not just the first time around. Doak writes:

> In recent years our architects spend millions to enclose and define every shot with mounds while smoothing down every bump in the fairways, attempting to eliminate blind shots and bad bounces from the game. The whole point of golf architecture is to discover and then present to the player challenging shots inherent in the landscape. But today anything remotely challenging is quickly criticized as "unfair." A green which tilts slightly away from the line of play is a natural challenge unto itself, but many golfers are so accustomed to having all the greens tilted back toward them to "receive a shot" that they believe a fall-away green is a gimmick.

The millions of dollars frequently spent to create "bowl" settings are justified by modern architects because those features supposedly speed up play and make golf more pleasurable. But the end result has seen no increase in pace of play, even with the help of golf carts. Worse, golfers are not required to make the tricky decisions that come with naturally wide holes that are defended by tilted or contoured greens requiring a certain angle of approach. The lack of naturalness in design also means golfers don't have a chance to create "feel" shots that naturally contoured holes such as the thirteenth at Augusta National call for.

Besides being more enjoyable to play, natural and strategic designs also bring relief to golfers' pocketbooks. With course construction costs for synthetic courses frequently pushing the $20 million mark (due in large part to poor site selection and expensive theatrics), the green-fee customer has to pay for the architect's desire to rearrange land unsuited for golf. Further, several studies have found that many Americans would like to play golf but do not for three primary reasons: high green fees, excessive difficulty, and pace of play. All of these barriers have direct ties to modern golf architecture trends.

Many of today's architects and developers declare that golfers are getting the type of courses they demand. Maybe they do, but some golfers do not know what makes a golf course fun, nor do they understand the value of classic design principles. Certain architects know how to balance the needs of all levels of play and all types of egomaniacal developers without compromising their beliefs or the defining principles of golf architecture. Today, it's tough to find architects who know how to assess all of the requirements necessary to build a classic course and even tougher to build a classic with equipment advances looming over them.

WHY CAN'T THEY NAME THEM LIKE THEY USED TO?

"Naming rights. These should belong to parents, not corporations."

—JAMIE COURT, *CORPORATEERING*

Major League Baseball owners accepted $3.6 million from Sony Studios to slap "Spiderman" logos on stadium bases that were hosting games over a June 2004 weekend. The same June weekend that coincided with the release of *Spiderman 2*. Baseball's chief operating officer rebutted a small group of nitpickers by claiming that the move didn't detract from the game, but instead, "adds to the entertainment value."

Suddenly overwhelmed by millions of complaining "purists," baseball modified the deal within 24 hours and left its bases unmolested. For now, anyway.

Proponents of pervasive corporate advertising in sports will point to NASCAR. Some NASCAR fans claim that such pervasive product plugging is simply part of that pastime. Apparently, to them just watching the high-speed races is merely interesting. But, turn the cars into 200-mph billboard advertisements and now the races have tons of character!

But here's the really sad news: Golf is next.

To enhance "entertainment value," some course owners will do more than install tee signs sponsored by the local hardware store. You may soon see revenue-desperate courses auctioning off their names.

Get ready for Rogaine Ridge, Clorox Creek, and Levitra Lakes. Or The Experience at T Mobile Ranch Golf Club.

According to the spokesman for a northern California–based company brokering naming rights, this new income "can be passed on to the consumer either through better course maintenance or lower green fees."

The spokesman prefaced that side-splitter by telling *Golf World*, "should the course owner be so inclined, of course."

Yes, of course. We all know where that new income will go—straight to the owner's pocketbook. Hey, they're entitled. It's their course and their name. But just don't insult us by claiming this revenue will be passed along to the golfer.

For those involved with big-time tournament courses, brace yourselves for a different kind of commercialism. Within the next few years, expect to be mowing or painting logos, or more likely even constructing architectural "platforms" for the purpose of digital projection.

How come? That thing called TiVo.

TiVo and other similar digital video recorders work like an amazing high-tech VCR, recording programs digitally and, in general, making televised golf tolerable again. Armed with a TiVo remote, the viewer can fast forward through the excessive number of commercial breaks necessitated by huge purses, declining ratings, and corporate greed.

Now that TiVo is affordable ($100 for a 40-hour recorder, $13 a month for the service), golf fans will have a blast watching the final round in about 30 minutes.

Here comes a dreaded interview with the senior vice president of Brand Platform Cross-Polarization and Synchronicity to tell us what a great week his company had despite the rain-induced Monday finish, low attendance, and cranky winner.

No thanks. Fast forward.

I "TiVo'd" the final round of a recent event. I wasn't going to watch it, but heard something amazing happened. So I flew through the first 2 hours of commercials and missed the senior vice president's contractually obligated interview.

Then, I got to see Craig Parry's sudden-death playoff eagle. No commercials. No annoying product plugs. Just a few goose bumps.

When tournament sponsors go home and TiVo through events they've put $8 million into, they're going to start asking how they can avoid being TiVo'd.

Look for some enterprising PGA Tour vice president (Lord knows there are plenty of them) to suggest that fairways, bunkers, and greens be employed to ease the multimillion-dollar sponsorship blow.

We may see fairway mowing patterns subtly crafted into a shape resembling a sponsor logo. Or, how about bunkers in the shape of products? It's already been done at Disney World.

During a recent "prime-time" golf exhibition, a company paid for a closest-to-the-pin promotion. The company logo and a circle were digitally placed on the screen.

Why not just paint an ad on the putting surfaces so the camera has no choice but to beam the billboard into TV sets across the land? That way the gallery can soak up the brand all day long. It's only grass; it'll grow back. Most of all, some tour official will insist that golf's entertainment value was increased.

Right. And I've got some nice linksland on the Gaza Strip I'd love to sell you.

THE POLITICS OF DESIGN

ARMCHAIR ARCHITECTS AND THE DAMAGE THEY INFLICT

*"**Politics**, n. A strife of interests masquerading as a contest of principles."*
—AMBROSE BIERCE

When amateur golf architect George Thomas and his engineer sidekick Billy Bell built Riviera Country Club in 1926, they had one constant annoyance: developer Frank Garbutt, who didn't play golf or know anything about it. That did not stop Garbutt from visiting the site regularly and offering architectural suggestions for each hole.

Since Thomas was providing his services for free, he didn't have to listen to Garbutt. But instead of insulting the generous developer by telling him to "bugger off," Thomas and Bell talked to each other nonstop whenever Garbutt visited, never allowing the golf architecture–challenged client to get a word in. Eventually, Garbutt stopped making site visits.

Times have changed in golf—sort of. There are no practicing amateur architects like Thomas and there are only a handful of designers who have the clout to overrule problematic clients without fear of being fired. In most cases, the client's ideas become the focal point of most projects regardless of the client's architecture background or lack thereof. It is similar to the situation in which green committees naively overrule superintendents and then blame everyone but themselves when course conditions decline.

Modern course design involves a volatile mix of clashing egos, miscommunication, artistic beliefs, maintainability, length, and politics. All converge on the architect while the dirt is moved and rarely to the betterment of a project. This power struggle goes on because, unlike a building or home design that relies on precise engineering and city codes, a golf course can theoretically be built and maintained to some degree no matter how many odd ideas are injected into the design. A house built under these conditions would collapse before it was even habitable.

The balance between client involvement and architectural wisdom has tipped so far in the client's favor that most new golf courses open having cost millions more than necessary.

Several architects have shared their horror stories, all off the record out of fear that even the mention of their names will be used against them by future clients and architects. In hindsight, many of these tales are humorous. Others are disturbing, considering what's at stake. But as superintendents, managers, professionals, contractors, and architects find out all too often, golf course jobs depend on who treads most carefully through a set of land mines laid out by developers who usually are doing their first, and often their last, golf project.

One architect who deals with overseas projects offered several stories of his worst client nightmares. There was the "Chinese fellow who didn't want any par 4s because four in Chinese means death. Par 8s are good though, they mean prosperity—the more par 8s on the course the better. Then there was the client who insisted on 'combining French Renaissance garden design philosophy with golf course architecture.' That was interesting, too."

We've all heard of clubs infatuated with memorial tree programs, but one famous club that desperately seeks a U.S. Open told the visiting USGA staff it wouldn't cut down problematic trees (nor even trim them) because the owner believes human souls are entrenched in their bark. They have since relented in a desperate quest to attract a U.S. Open.

Another successful architect mentioned a client who, "on the first hole, complained bitterly about the fairway bunker [we built] on the right— saying it shouldn't be there because everyone sliced. I felt pretty confident he would like the second hole, with its fairway bunker left. But when he saw it, he said 'Why put a fairway bunker [on the] left, if no one ever hits there?'"

A popular and highly respected architect recounted this typical development nightmare: "One day, the money-half of the partners was making

PART FIVE

a rare site visit. As we walked the holes, I tried to give him a play-by-play of what was going on and what the finished product was going to look like. When we got to a par 3, I figured there was no way our tour could not brighten, especially with such a naturally wonderful golf hole. I explained that the back tee played to about 185 yards and the angle of the wetland bank favored a right-to-left shot. Pointing out the first peninsula, I showed how the angle was less difficult and the distance on the hole was reduced to about 140 yards [from the middle tee]. Then on to the last tee setting and a hole of about 105 yards. I then turned to the money guy, expecting him to toss me at least a little crumb, and he tersely asked, 'Why so many tees?'

"Only mildly flustered, I waded right in with the typical stuff about par 3s and players of various abilities and playing lengths and angles and all that stuff. I went on for 3 or 4 minutes only to again be greeted with—in an even more terse delivery—'Why so many tees?'"

The architect continues, "I then got more direct, something to the effect of, it's a par 3 . . . people take divots . . . you need the extra space for the turf to repair itself . . . and so on and so forth. Giving new meaning to terseness, the money man said—in a totally serious fashion—'Why don't you just use a rubber mat?' With no further words, we moved on to the next hole."

THE REALITY OF RANKINGS

"The reason for the survival of the award system is purely commercial."

—ROBERT HENRI

There comes a time when each of us concludes that the various "Top 100" lists are taken too seriously. The first time I sensed something was amiss came when visiting the pro shop of a great old course, only to find they had embroidered their current *Golf Digest* ranking on every cap for sale: #83.

However, it was apparent that rankings had transcended rationality when a frustrated architect reported that the "restoration" project he wanted to undertake had become an excuse for club members to "toughen up" their course. The emphasis had shifted from bringing back the classic architecture to shoring up the course's "resistance to scoring" characteristics.

Why?

The members felt that a tougher course was their only way to a higher position on *Golf Digest*'s "America's 100 Greatest" list, a ranking that unaccountably includes the ballot category "resistance to scoring."

The rankings obsession has degenerated to the point that the jobs of architects, superintendents, and management personnel can depend on how a course is perceived by ranking panelists. This is a sad situation indeed, considering that at best, the panelists and their various lists merely give us something to talk about. But at their (frequent) worst, the rankings are created with either too much or too little criteria, and voted on by panelists who either don't know how to distinguish ordinary golf holes from great ones, or who visit a course once and miss out on the subtleties.

Let's take a closer look at the two major rankings so that at least you know what you are getting into.

GOLF DIGEST'S "AMERICA'S 100 GREATEST" AND "BEST NEW" LISTS

Golf Digest proclaimed in 1999 that their list was the original and oldest ranking (true). They also patted themselves on the back for being the most open and consistent regarding voting procedures and criteria (also true). Yet, the panel consistently seems to ignore what architecture editor Ron Whitten preaches in his writings by emphasizing conditioning, aesthetics, and "resistance to scoring."

The best-defined category on the *Digest* ballot, "playability," counts only in balloting for its biannual listing of the best public courses, even though panelists award a playability score for each course they see. Now, consider this definition of "playability": "How well does the course challenge the low handicap golfers while still providing enjoyable options for high handicappers through the use of shorter lengths, alternative routes, placement of hazards, and accessible pins?"

Your basic timeless course design.

And, an evaluation of those elements doesn't count for their listing of greatest courses!

The *Digest* panel is unique, however, in having a higher annual growth rate than most Fortune 500 companies. In 1999 the panel reached 660 members, up from 577 in 1997 and up from 450 in 1995. Now, it's nearing 1,000.

Described as well-traveled, "publicity-shy, low-handicappers," the magazine unintentionally gives the impression that they have created a frat-house buddy system to gain access to America's best courses. Several panelists regret the image *Digest* paints, or perhaps just remember when *Golf Digest* proudly revealed in print that they awarded a position to one panelist as a 50th birthday present.

The *Golf Digest* ballot consists of seven categories that require a 1-to-10 score, 10 being highest: "shot values," "playability," "resistance to scoring," "design variety," "memorability," "esthetics," and "conditioning."

The mysterious shot values category counts double in the final tally, while playability is eliminated and conditioning is tinkered with in some way that wisely softens the blow of an off-maintenance day.

Once the scores are tallied, two points are added for courses that allow walking, while no points are awarded if carts are mandatory. However, panelists are not required to walk the courses they rate, and rarely do— another major flaw among all panelists regardless of the magazine they represent. (Although, if recent trends continue, "cart path camouflage" will be a future category.)

There is, however, one ever-so-important saving grace for the *Golf Digest* Top 100: the "tradition" category. This score is tacked on by a mysterious in-house committee once the panelists have weighed in on America's toughest and prettiest courses.

Consider these 1999 editorial modifications, which are typical of the biannual plastic surgery undertaken by "the editors." Prior to the tradition score, Wade Hampton came in at no. 8 in America but moved to no. 22 in the final published ranking. Shadow Creek ranked no. 6 in the panelists' eyes, but moved to no. 20 on the official list. (It has plummeted further in subsequent rankings.). Colorado's Sanctuary Golf Club landed at a stunning no. 17, before the in-house committee dropped it down to no. 48.

However, thanks to the tradition score (and I mean it in these cases), Baltimore Country Club went from the panelists' no. 84 to a more respectable no. 50. Classy Kittansett Club starts at no. 71 but got moved to a more reasonable no. 39. Baltusrol (Lower) went from a surprising no. 62, to a more logical post-tradition no. 34 on the published list. And thanks to the editors, Riviera Country Club surged from no. 52 to no. 24 in the published ranking.

Why does the *Digest* panel produce results that force the editors to correct their findings so drastically? Perhaps because they have too many low handicappers voting. Like tour players, most good golfers focus on what *they* shot or how "fair" the course seemed to *them*, instead of analyzing the design and how interesting it is for *all* players. Thus, courses they deem "easy" get downgraded.

PART FIVE

You ask, who cares about what some publicity-shy rich guy thinks is a good "test" of golf? Just tell us which are the best *designs*, right? Anyone can make a course difficult. Tell us which courses are the most fun for the most people. Tell us which are the most thought-provoking, timeless layouts. Please stop giving points for layouts perceived as extraordinarily "pretty." And don't give excessive weight to the service you got on the one day you played. A course should not be penalized a point because the superintendent decided to not mow the green collars the lone day one of *Golf Digest's* thousands, err, hundreds of panelists happened to test how resistant to scoring the course was.

GOLF MAGAZINE'S TOP 100 COURSES IN THE U.S.

Intentionally opposite to *Golf Digest*, *Golf Magazine's* list of the Top 100 U.S. layouts employs vague—and for many years the self-indulgent "I know it when I see it"—criterion for judging. (Thankfully, the last two *Golf Magazine* lists have not cited the "I know it when I see it" approach in print.) The all-about-me method is a dangerously subjective attitude for evaluating the greatest designs, especially with a small panel where a vote here or there can affect people's livelihood.

There are no criteria when voting for *Golf Magazine's* list, just an "A to F" grading system for their 100 panelists to use in summing up what they like and don't like. For a long time there were no recommendations to study the effect of the routing or to assess the placement of tees, bunkers, or trees. Just tell us what you think because you are special and you know greatness when you see it.

A few of these topics are now recommended for study, earning *Golf Magazine* serious bonus points for at least trying to put the focus back on architecture.

While the *Golf Digest* panel overemphasizes elements they should not be overemphasizing, *Golf Magazine* creates debatable results by not asking their panelists to analyze and rate *any* specific elements of a design. *Golf Magazine's* list, like *Golf Digest's*, is notorious for its infatuation with certain new courses or USGA venues, only to turn on them a few years

142

later (e.g., Troon North, Kiawah Island Ocean Course, Wild Dunes, Haig Point, Bellerive).

Golf Magazine, featuring a panel that is stocked with designers, developers, USGA staffers, tour players, and even a PR rep for several architects, raises conflict of interest questions that undermine the process.

Adding a few criteria and a few more panel members would help cut down on the conflict questions. Also, *Golf Magazine's* panel was down to a mere eighty-six voters in 2003. That means some courses on the list got as few as five votes to earn their ranking, and with someone like architect Rees Jones able to vote on courses he has redesigned for a U.S. Open, you can see why the results might be easily questioned. (Torrey Pines, no. 67 in America in 2003?)

These lists will always be fun, goofy, inexplicable, and largely the panelists' flavor of the month. The Top 100 lists have been beneficial to the golf business by raising the standing of courses, bringing recognition to excellent designs while improving the stature of architects and superintendents.

However, the lists carry too much clout considering their inexact systems. Too many panelists are in it to play free golf instead of to analyze the best design work. The rankings have little effect on what really matters: how much people enjoy the courses they play, regardless of ranking.

Worst of all, rankings now influence people's livelihoods. No, the magazines did not set out to make them this weighty, but now that the lists are so popular, the panels and criteria should be more closely monitored and refined.

Architects and superintendents are pressured to create something "great" in order to be ranked by a few too many people who don't know what great is. Developers spend millions to top the course down the street in hopes of landing on the "Best New" lists. Meanwhile, the rankings and their panelists are no longer just a little strange; they are a little dangerous.

WHAT'S IN A SIGNATURE?

". . . a dreadful cliché that probably has done as much harm as any phrase I can recall."

—Tom Fazio on signature design, 2000

"We want all the shots at Berkeley Hall to be signature shots . . ."

—Tom Fazio, 2001

If you don't like manufactured-looking layouts and are tired of architects' ideas regurgitated from course to course, blame it on "signature design."

The use of "signature" apparently implies that the presence of a famous professional confers an automatic stamp of quality and in some cases, instant renown for the latest and greatest design. But with several hundred courses opening every year and only a handful making a mark on anyone's radar screen, we are finding out that the celebrity signature is meaningless for indicating whether the architecture is any good. The only thing it consistently means is that you're going to pay a lot of money to play.

Signature designs have come to mean that an architect was paid at least $1 million to give a client the same look he gave another course in the neighborhood. The big name signature is supposed to have the same comforting effect that a major corporate identity such as Hertz or Marriott gives to travelers. The name tells them what to expect: consistency and reliability.

But do we want all of our golf courses to look and play alike? Or do we want variety, intrigue, and something unexpected?

One dictionary defines "signature" as "a distinctive mark, characteristic, or sound effect indicating identity." Yet only a few "signature" design firms actually work with the land and blend their designs into the landscape to the point that we can barely tell the architects were even there.

In reality, most design firms move dirt around and eliminate native plant material to stamp their style on the site regardless of the natural surroundings. That is not working with nature. It's leaving a mark—and usually a not-so-attractive one at that.

The signature design term started in earnest when the late Robert Trent Jones Sr. began to sign advertisements in his own handwriting. His courses soon came to be recognized as the result of his signature design work. A simple marketing ploy turned into an excuse for architects to stay in their offices and whip out signature plans.

From there, like so many design fads, the term gradually spread until it has become a costly disease of epidemic proportions. The term is even repeated with regularity by television announcers who refer to imaginary things like the "front nine signature hole." Ugh.

Y7K?

"We read that for the next Open Championship Hoylake is to be over 7,000 yards long; such stretching of the course may be necessary, but it is not in the least cheering to hear of; it opens up no real way out of the difficulty. Perhaps there is no way, but, if there is, it lies in doing something to the ball and not to the course."

—BERNARD DARWIN, 1936

Yours truly attended a media day for yet another overpriced golf course under construction. Several writers and photographers fawned over the architect and asked vital questions such as, "Is this the best site you've ever had to work with?"

The architect said it was. Most believed him even though he has built courses along ocean cliffs, while this place was being carved through steep, rattlesnake-infested canyons.

As the media tour proceeded, a magazine photographer looked over a colorful map of the design. In an alarmed tone, he posed a question to the course's marketing guru after we had left the architect.

"I see the course is par 72, but it's only 6,935 yards from the tips," he said, implying that the course lacked relevancy because it failed to clear the 7,000-yard plateau.

"Oh, it's over 7,000 now," the marketing person reassured us in a moment of rapid spin control. Lord knows what they did to get to 7,000, but it probably didn't involve a newly constructed tee. They probably just used an eraser.

The notion that credibility comes only to a golf course with a back tee yardage over 7,000 continues to be one of the more shallow "standards" in modern golf. Many say there is a retro movement in golf architecture, with the 7,000-yard requirement an outdated concept. But in the face of technology advancements and our nation's obsession with big numbers, the 7,000-yard standard is probably more pervasive than ever. There is little hope of turning back to the 6,300-yard plateau that people like Donald Ross and Bobby Jones felt should be the maximum length of any course hoping to provide a pleasurable round in a reasonable amount of time.

Marketing forces have seized upon the 7,000-yard mentality. The American golfing public continues to believe that a new course is only worthwhile if it is a par-72/7,000-yard "championship" design. Anything less just doesn't offer full value, even if the golfer in question never sets foot on the 7,000-yard tees.

The 7,000-yard plateau plagues golf the same way the 1970s gave birth to concrete multipurpose sports stadiums that were based on the notion of bigger-is-better. They could hold huge crowds and house several types of sporting events.

Imagine telling an architect to design a golf course so that it can hold downhill skiing events in the winter. Or telling him to shape features so that the course operator can host the occasional motocross championship at the expense of prime seating for the baseball games that will be played there eighty-one times a year.

Dreary places like Veterans Stadium in Philadelphia and Riverfront Stadium in Cincinnati were created to be useful for a variety of events. Each of these cold places could seat a lot of people, but that was about all they did. It's not a coincidence they have been demolished within 40 years of their creation.

Thankfully, baseball is enjoying a "retro" movement with quirkier, more intimate, fan-friendly parks in vogue. But genuine retro has happened at only a few golf courses. We have a greater understanding of the classic courses than ever, yet there is the persistent belief that only a course topping a certain yardage is truly of "championship" quality. What nonsense.

Consider this. The top four courses in America are typically the same in the three most popular "Top 100" rankings. They are Pebble Beach, Cypress Point, Shinnecock Hills, and Pine Valley. Average back tee yardage: 6,800 yards, and that average is boosted by the addition of yardage from rarely used U.S. Open tees at Shinnecock and Pebble Beach.

Golf needs to emulate baseball's retro movement by incorporating charming irregularities and even downright quirkiness into course designs. The focus should be on having a variety of holes with an emphasis on the return of at least two short, do-or-die par 4s per eighteen, and preferably three. (Short par 4s really put a dent in the attempt to reach the 7,000-yard mark, which is why they are always the first to get left out.)

Of course, if golf had done something about the ball back when the architects were griping in the 1920s and 1930s, we would now have 6,200-yard courses that would be much less costly to maintain, much faster to play, and likely more fun than the prevailing 7,000-yard giants.

Not content with 7,000 yards, we are pushing the 7,500-yard barrier now, with 8,000 yards in sight for new courses.

As one of those wise old architects said, "Length means nothing without character." But length means a lot when it comes to cost, time, and interest.

BLINDING!

"They have a strange color to the sand out here, it's not that beautiful white stuff. Sort of a rust color."
                                            —JOHNNY MILLER, 2003 U.S. OPEN TELECAST

Just when you think golf is making progress in its bid to better fit into our environment, along comes another toxic substance to create headaches for those dedicated folks who are trying to make the game affordable and environmentally friendly. This particular element causes a glaring problem (literally), by giving environmentalists easy ammunition to say, "see, golf just doesn't give a damn about blending in."

Don't know what I'm talking about? Hint: It requires the use of 45 or higher UVA/UVB sunscreen within 15 feet of its wrath. UVA ray protective sunglasses are necessary, too.

Yes, it's fluorescent bunker sand.

Has there ever been a more garish, costly, or offensive trend in golf than the recent widespread popularity of blinding white bunker sand? Has any fad ever arrived on the golf scene that has so captivated golfers for such unknown reasons?

Well, there were those orange-colored golf balls for a while, but even they look cool and classy compared to the blinding grains of silica.

One Southern California course requires its staff to wear sunglasses when raking bunkers. The rule was instituted after—yes, that's right, an innocent bunker-raker had to be treated for snow-blindness! (*Note*: Snow-blindness is defined as a temporary or partial loss of sight caused when the eyes are directly exposed to the sun's ultraviolet light reflected off snow or ice. Or in this poor lad's case, bunker sand.)

Besides being dangerous to the eyes, not particularly attractive, and definitely offensive to non golfers, white sand has taken on financial significance for courses. Using the *really* white stuff means at least *double* and usually *triple* the cost just to get it out of the quarry and onto the property.

On top of the excessive cost to buy and dye the sparkly stuff, there's the pricey bunker lining that most architects and superintendents recommend to keep the white dust clean. And in areas where the frosty fill can't be easily found (which is just about everywhere except Cape Cod and Carmel), Dolimitic Lime is added at additional cost and effort to turn natural white into blinding white. The Dolimitic dyeing process has to be repeated yearly to keep things bleachy.

It's a grotesque waste of money and resources.

Yet, some golfers inexplicably crave this tacky stuff like pathetic junkies. Or at least the golf business thinks so, and thus is eager to provide the fix.

Timeless designs blend into their surrounding environment to give a golfer the feeling of battling nature. It's sort of like the thrill people say they experience while fishing or hunting: just you versus Mother Nature. In other words, the best-looking layouts don't put in brown "waste areas" to contrast with the white bunkers, as all too many new courses do for intentional *contrast*.

Incorporating blinding white bunker sand into environments where it didn't exist is not only expensive, but it also takes away that enchanted feeling of playing in a native setting. Worse, it says to the world, "We don't care what anyone else thinks."

Is that a statement golf can afford to make?

SMALL GREENS ARE OVERRATED

"It has often been said that architects have designs for eighteen greens and that the same ones are used over and over again on the various layouts. A successful architect of today does not follow that system. His greens are born on the ground and made to fit each particular hole."

—WILLIAM FLYNN

There is one particularly irritating form of revisionist golf architecture history that keeps getting in the way of sound course restoration work. It's the belief that small greens were the old-time architects' best ally, and thus, small greens must be a sign of sound design in any era.

After all, big greens can't be any good. They're too easy to hit with today's equipment. The old architects surely knew this would happen and designed accordingly.

Wrong!

History tells us that master designers like MacKenzie and Tillinghast designed greens on the small side. The telltale sign of genius is found in green size. Big greens are for average courses; small equals greatness.

The old architects did *not* design "small" greens. And they certainly never celebrated small greens as the measure of quality, something to be emulated. Only occasionally did they build a green under 3,500 square feet.

Even with plenty of evidence showing how things used to be, we still hear golf announcers remark that tiny greens have that "old style" and character. And there are plenty of everyday golfers who insist that saucer-plate putting surfaces make their course the masterpiece that it is.

With technology making the sport easier to play, small greens are regarded as a pre-emptive strike against players using shorter irons for their approach shots.

COST SPIKE: A LOOK AT GREEN CONSTRUCTION

When trying to figure out why newer courses lack the subtlety of older courses, even a novice architecture critic can tell that the greens on older layouts "feel" different. They seem smaller, the contours feel more natural, and they tend to blend in more comfortably with their surroundings.

This is due to the advent of the "USGA green" and the intricacy of its subsurface drainage system that allows faster green speeds. To build such a green is far more complicated than the old "push-up" green built out of native soils, still found at many older courses.

If a course is built on porous soil, the cost of a push-up green can cost as little as 50¢ per square foot to build, while a USGA green will run around $6 per square foot to

---

But having too many small greens undermines the character of a course. They make it impossible for significant contours to be built, and the absence of significant square footage eliminates space for unique hole locations that would add day-to-day variety.

Increased variety and additional options make golfers think, and we all know that thinking makes the game more difficult (in a fun way). And true exhilaration in golf comes from figuring out how to overcome difficulties and actually pulling off the shot you imagined.

Sure, it's fun to approach a small, tightly bunkered green complex once in a while. Two or maybe three under 4,500 square feet can spice things up. But besides the obvious maintenance benefits of larger greens, it is fun to play on well-designed surfaces that offer as many as ten distinct hole locations. A quick bit of research reveals that many classic green complexes once had fascinating corner hole locations, since lost over time to poor mowing practices or modification by clueless committees. Often these original green sizes are not restored because golfers believe their course is superior thanks to their petite greens.

The small-green myth has taken on even greater significance as

construct. An average-sized green typically covers 6,000 square feet.

A modified version of the USGA method, called the "California" green, starts around $2 per square foot and has become a more popular version to construct because it allows architects more design freedom and does not require the intricate matching of subsurface layers that the USGA green demands.

Debates rage in the golf construction and maintenance fields over which method is best, but there is little doubt that architecture and value for the golfer have been affected by the cost of a USGA green, regardless of how well it functions. Many golfers are willing to pay the price if it means their superintendents can keep greens alive in the race to achieve lightning-fast greens.

modern architects struggle to build large putting surfaces with subtle character. Most modern greens are bulky, clumsily popping up out of the fairway like a tombstone. The precise construction requirements of the "USGA green" deserve some of the blame (the contours of the green surface must be matched at each layer below). Combine that with target golf and the rush to get courses built as soon as possible, and you see a lack of artistry or subtlety in modern green design.

The trick is to create a putting surface in the 7,000-square-foot range and make it seem small. Course designers Bill Coore and Ben Crenshaw recently achieved this at Hidden Creek Golf Club near Atlantic City. Superintendent Jeff Riggs has an average of 8,000 square feet of putting surface to maintain, yet the greens don't look or play nearly that large. The contours are bold but stretch out gently, and the greens tie in beautifully to the fairways, disguising their size.

Pay no attention to good golfers who insist that small putting surfaces make a design better. Bigger makes for more interesting golf when it comes to putting surfaces.

A THING UNTO ITSELF

"Each hole must be a thing unto itself!"

—ANONYMOUS

We've all heard golfers proclaim the importance of trees and other assorted oddities employed to separate holes. It's almost as if the each-hole-unto-itself philosophy has some ancient biblical foundation. Perhaps it's Shakespearean.

That's it! A lost scene from "Hamlet," set in a contentious green committee meeting. After hours of laborious debate, one of the pro-tree planting characters jumps from his seat, waves his fist in a fury, and screams, "Thou shalt not tolerate such bland aesthetics; each hole must be a thing unto itself! Thou shalt plant trees for separation, no matter where the place!"

Golfers have believed for too long that great courses are respectable because each of their eighteen holes sits by its lonesome self. Each hole must be free of views of other golfers, even if it means lining the rear of a green with a straight row of spruces. The "we must not see other golfers from our hole" mentality has killed more turf and ruined more interesting holes than any other single architectural theory in golf.

Ironically, the very same golfers who want to plant a lot of trees or who fight to keep unnecessary trees around usually happen to be the very same golfers who sit in the locker room playing cards, oblivious to Mr. Havercamp and his leathery body walking naked from the showers to his locker. The sight of men who bypass the towel rack and bare all for the world apparently is not offensive? Yet it's apocalyptic when you can see a threesome over on the eighth fairway while you putt out on the fourth green?

LAS VEGAS SHOWGIRL DESIGN

A retired superintendent, Randy Wilson, writes a monthly column for *Golfweek's Superintendent News*. In the November 7, 2003, issue, he summed up the beauty of Ben Crenshaw and Bill Coore's many subtle modern designs and described what too many modern "signature" designs remind him of: Las Vegas showgirls! Wilson wrote:

> Crenshaw is gently steering us away from 'Las Vegas Showgirl' design, the philosophy that stresses excessive cosmetics, outrageous feathery costumes and artificial, surgically enhanced mounding. While the initial appeal of the showgirl is undeniable, she is an expensive date, a poor long-term prospect and not what we would bring home to meet Mother. We can grow old with the sweet and wholesome girl-next-door, the rough and tumble tomboy who needs little makeup to look good and enjoys the simpler things. The showgirl will abandon us at the first sign of financial weakness.
>
> It's time to thank Crenshaw for helping us rediscover the sweet and wholesome designs and keeping us from the tempting allure, the siren call of the showgirl golf course.

The each-hole-unto-itself virus has infected golfers because of the influence of a select group of ignorant architects whose design philosophy centers on the belief that hole-to-hole privacy is vital to happiness and peace on earth.

The obsession with plugging every visible gap to satisfy the sacred each-hole-unto-itself dictum is costly and makes golf less fun to play by restricting playing corridors and blocking attractive views. More trees also make it tougher to grow grass.

So if it's not Shakespearean in origin, where did this mistaken idea originate? Some blame the creator of Pine Valley.

Supposedly, one of George Crump's reasons for building Pine Valley was his desire "to keep every hole free of view of any other." Yet, at great expense he cut down every tree and dug up the roots as construction started. But, somehow it has become "gospel" that the world's premier course is the best because each hole is by itself as the architect intended. Actually that's the *least* interesting aspect of its magnificent design. Recently, the club has been removing trees where Crump did not want them.

Today, thanks to the educational efforts of many superintendents and architects, golfers are beginning to understand that trees used as frames merely make courses claustrophobic, overly penal, and more expensive to maintain.

Fairway is returning to land previously covered by trees. Holes are no longer things unto themselves, and guess what? The game not only survives, but it also improves when the trees come out.

Mature native trees, once screened from view, can now be appreciated for their beauty and the way they punctuate an open course. Turf is allowed to grow again. Golf can actually be played as it was meant to be. Best of all, golfers are learning that the sun will still rise in the east and set in the west after you remove a few superfluous trees.

Now, if we could do something about those naked men strolling through the locker room, we'd be making real progress.

PART VI

RESTORING GOLF'S CHARACTER

"Frequent visits to Scotland and among our home courses have convinced me that the time is ripe for a stupendous revision looking toward a saner and simpler plan for turning the good earth into playgrounds for those who follow through."

—PERRY MAXWELL, ARCHITECT OF SOUTHERN HILLS AND PRAIRIE DUNES

To have a healthy future, golf must put an end to technology-boosted distance increases that result from outsmarting regulation. Actually, putting a stop to the manufacturers' reign would lessen the overall emphasis placed on consuming the latest equipment and might even lift the choke hold on architectural elements that make golf fun and affordable. In essence, golf would be taken back from the manufacturers.

Since a distance rollback will be tough, if not impossible, let us consider alternative ways to solve the issue. Something has to change, otherwise the never-ending arms race that benefits only a few manufacturers will continue to lead to longer courses, narrower fairways, smaller greens, more rough, more expensive rounds, and other mechanisms that will leave golf's future in doubt.

Yes, some golfers will grumble about no longer having the chance of gaining distance with the simple act of whipping out a credit card, but if they see that the benefits could be more enjoyable, affordable, and faster rounds, wouldn't they embrace the concept? And if the focus returns to interesting architecture as opposed to hit-and-hope courses that have been over-rigged to combat a constantly changing sport, won't that make golf more appealing?

Topics here include the impact of handicapping, the need for a golf "think tank," the return of the stymie, ways to revamp the USGA, letting kids caddy, the need for more "native golf," the possible classic public-course restoration movement, and a plea to reassess our values. The following topics are offered in the spirit of discussion and provocation. With productive dialogue, the future can unfold in a productive manner.

THE CONCERN OF THE ARCHITECT (THEN, NOW, AND BEYOND)

"The concern of the architect . . . is not that of a moralist, the principal word of whose vocabulary is DON'T."

—MAX BEHR, 1927

There is something peculiar about people (men, mostly) referring to the importance of "defending" or "protecting par." Augusta National chairman Hootie Johnson is sounding like a politician, repeatedly proclaiming his determination to restore "a premium on accuracy," as if his handlers told him to ingrain this mantra into our heads so eventually we'll believe it.

I find it unseemly when spectators talk about how a tough course "put the players in their place" by embarrassing them, as opposed to producing an exciting display of excellent golf, allowing golfers to show off their skill.

The approach to golf, both professional and recreational, has become pessimistic. Putting players in their place is an almost sadistic view of what our grounds for golf should do. Anyone can make a golf course impossible and put a "premium on accuracy." The real art is to make it difficult, but reasonable. Challenging, but beatable by a smart, crafty shot maker.

The state of golf is exemplified in the stiff-upper-lip reaction some golfers feel they must demonstrate after they've finished an absolutely miserable day on the links. A day, for example, that consisted of lost balls and deteriorating skill, fueled by the apprehension of playing penal holes. But the golfer dutifully gives a nod to the course and says, "Boy, it's a good, tough test."

159

If they were to point out that the course was too penal or too hard or took too bloody long to play, they would sound like whiners, even though they would be telling the truth.

The golf industry is finding out the hard way that penal designs compel many folks to take up bird-watching or some other less stressful and less expensive pastime.

The idea that a golf course and its architect should serve as administers of justice will not help the sport grow. Golf courses should be places where the golfer can show off his talent, both mental and physical. But such a design bothers some people because those courses occasionally permit birdies, reward good play, or even permit luck. Perish the thought!

In an era when technology has such a strong influence, attempts to keep golfers humbly thrilled with "par" have led to the creation of ever more penal and dull golf courses. If distance goes unregulated, architects will continually be asked to counteract unregulated technology with penal design ploys, while needing more acres to keep players safe.

If we ever wonder why so many golfers quit the sport or play less often, we should ask whether the current architecture fads reward the free, independent style of golf that lets us slash away. But at the end of the fairway, does the hole feature a green that rewards the thinking shot maker who placed his tee shot better than the slasher?

Watching the plodding U.S. Open–style of golf reminds us that there is a huge difference between a strategic golf course (like the Old Course at St. Andrews or the original Augusta National) and a penal course (like Oak Hill in 2003 or Carnoustie in 1999).

The strategic course gives the player enough rope to hang himself but also enough room to carve his own path to redemption. The penal seeks to whip, hang, and discipline the player from the first tee to the last. Hazing golf.

What makes it all the more disturbing is that there is a not-so-subtle example to learn from.

Golfers have been going to St. Andrews for a couple of hundred years now. What is the attraction? Max Behr wrote that St. Andrews provides "a spirit of conquest" where the golfer stamps "his law upon the ground."

THE CONCERN OF THE ARCHITECT
SHOULD BE POSITIVE . . .

In 1927, Max Behr spelled out the role of the architect. Here's Mr. Behr, uncut and uncensored:

> The concern of the architect should be positive and have solely to do with what the golfer should do. His mission is not that of a moralist the principal word of whose vocabulary is DON'T. The golfer should not be made to feel that he must renounce, that the primary object for him is to conquer his faults. It is not for the architect to inform him when he has played badly. That is the province of his professional. No, the mission of the architect is that of a leader. By the deployment of his hazards he exhorts the golfer to do his best, enticing him at times 'to shoot the bones for the whole works.' Thus he instills in the golfer a spirit of conquest by presenting him with definite objectives upon which he must concentrate. It is for the golfer to stamp his law upon the ground. It is in no way the business of the architect to stamp his law upon the golfer. But thus it is in most cases. The penal school of golf spells death to that spirit of independence, life and freedom which we are all seeking, and which we should find of all places in our recreations.

At St. Andrews there is a "spirit of independence, life and freedom which we are all seeking," and "which we should find of all places in our recreations."

Alister MacKenzie wrote that St. Andrews "is a course which caters to a higher standard of golf than any one has attained today, and yet it is extremely pleasurable to the old gentleman who cannot drive a ball any further than a lusty youth could kick one."

Not enough of our golf courses deliver even a fraction of the spirit that St. Andrews inspires. Give golfers decent width, interesting greens, and carefully placed bunkers, and you're bound to have something that will be fun to play. The architect should seek to present a challenge that can be overcome, not to prevent good play, but to encourage it.

MEMO: WE WANT TO WATCH GOLF, NOT CELEBRITIES

To: Network television executives
From: A. Viewer

How do I say this nicely? For the nearly $850 million you have been paying for PGA Tour rights through 2006, I think you deserve better. I know, golf (and all sports) can be justified as "loss leaders," that wonderful MBA-ism to justify a big money loser like you have on your hands with the current PGA Tour TV deal.

And yes, tour golfers are usually cooperative about doing interviews and in general, are humble, sensible athletes. But that doesn't necessarily pay the bills.

This golf you've been showing us and paying top dollar for is a watered down, power-heavy, sanitized version of the sport. And as fine as the golfers on the PGA Tour are, their wonderfulness will not sustain audiences over the long haul. Nor will it create new golfers or any passion for golf.

Don't believe me? Then why do your announcers spend so much time reminding us how great the golf is? I guess the incessant talking helps keep us awake through sometimes as few as two shots before the next commercial break. Not long ago we could watch a tournament, likely one directed by Frank Chirkinian at CBS, and the announcers were not promoting something every time they opened their mouth. It's one thing to be positive, another to be a cheerleader.

The 2003 ratings were down 6 percent overall, and the majors really took a hit. The PGA Championship final round was off 38 percent, the U.S. Open 44 percent. One million fewer people watched Phil Mickelson's 2004 win than the previous masters.

Yes, you can argue that ratings basically depend on whether Tiger is in contention or not. And yes, all sports ratings are down (well, except the NFL and NASCAR). However, golf will not retain its audience or grow in popularity by becoming a celebrity-watching session. These are not glitzy celebrities. They are nice, normal folks who, when you put them on a dynamic design that asks them to make tough risk-reward decisions, become incredible performers. When golf is in that special alignment where players must choose between enticing options and only the best are able to pull off the shot, that makes for rewarding—even thrilling—television.

Do the tours produce exciting golf that makes people want to watch when Tiger isn't playing? No. The tour has emphasized marketable celebrity watching over quality of sport.

Think about this when your contract is up for renewal and the commissioner asks for a cool $1 billion. Inform the folks at the PGA Tour you want more bang for your buck.

Here is what you tell them. Vary setups from week to week so that the focus returns to strategy and intelligence. This will help return architecture and shotmaking to the forefront, as will a return to venues that promote such golf over those that reward plodding play.

Power and technology do not make golf exciting to watch on television. It's certainly exciting in person to see John Daly or Hank Kuehne belt a long drive, but it's the creativity and decision-making scenarios that make golf on TV interesting to watch.

A tournament (shorter) ball would allow the better designs to breed excitement through tough decisions that ask players to deal with tricky risk-reward situations. Announcers can talk about these situations until they're blue in the face. Why? Because such scenarios are interesting. We've all faced them. We all know the feeling of not knowing which option to choose.

Of course, the few times these exciting situations come up these days, the announcers always seem to be talking in those rare moments the sound person is picking up what is being said between player and caddy. Oh joy!

Sorry, but the 1-minute interviews with tour players about their vacations or their new caddies or their chances of winning some award or their change to a Chevy this year (wait, wrong sport), well, it's all just not very interesting.

But watching someone struggle to decide whether to go for a par 5 in two while a roar comes from another part of the course? Now that is thrilling, cerebral, interactive—exactly why golf is the most complete of all sports. That will boost your beloved ratings and positively affect recreational golf, which in turn helps some of your sponsors.

Contrary to what some say, golf the everyday sport thrives when it's exciting to watch on television and when golfers can relate to the tough decisions the pros are asked to make.

THE CASE FOR THE CLASSIC COURSE BALL

"We believe that if the PGA Tour decides that it wants to regulate its members with a 'tour-spec ball,' we would be in favor of it. We have the same concerns about the record book and the sanctity of great old golf courses as they do."

—LARRY DORMAN, VICE PRESIDENT CALLAWAY GOLF

What is golf's greatest asset?

The politically correct, feel-good answer is obvious: the golfers. Without those devoted hackers in their sweat-stained bucket caps whizzing around in GPS-guided carts, there would be no golf. Right?

Well, without golf courses, there would be no place for those people to play. *Courses* are golf's greatest asset.

And how do governing bodies and golfers show their love for golf's architecture? By suggesting it's easier to alter real estate than rules.

What love.

These complicated venues are unique in the world of sport. Many are so beautiful and fascinating and enduring that they can legitimately be called works of art. Most are maintained to a daily standard considered unattainable not long ago.

The fine line between a course that functions as it was intended to and one that doesn't quite measure up is now blurred by constant distance increases. Owners of golf courses must adapt to changes in the sport while the United States Golf Association watches and supports this absurd notion. Many lovingly built and maintained courses—most of which served the sport admirably for decades—are supposedly letting us down because they can't withstand the assault from today's equipment.

But it's not just old courses that can't keep up.

PART SIX

One layout where a PGA Tour event was hosted in the fall of 2003 has already been lengthened (at the course owner's expense) in a mad race to keep up with this year's hot ball and driver. The course in question had not even been open for 1 year!

A BACK DOOR REVOLUTION?

"The seller of goods generally panders to the blind instincts of his customers. Rarely do we find him an artist considering what the result must be when his goods reach their destination. And the blind instinct that he catered to was an insane desire to merely hit the ball a long way."

—MAX BEHR, 1927

The $25 billion golf course industry (that's fees- and maintenance-industry sales combined) can separate itself from this long-ball nonsense and lay the groundwork for a future that emphasizes the joy of playing golf. The $4.5 billion equipment industry will no longer be in charge.

Golf professionals, superintendents, architects, administrators, and committee members who want to secure the sport's future can reverse the trend of declining rounds and courses expanding to accommodate an ever-changing sport. At the very least, they should start spreading the word that the sport itself can become paramount again.

How do we take golf back from the manufacturers? Look to Soft-spikes.

The golf course industry campaigned for and implemented the ban on metal spikes in order to improve turf conditions. More than 12,000 courses now ban metal spikes, and it started (apology for the pun) on a grass-roots level.

The same thing can happen with the golf ball: Introducing . . . the Classic Course Ball.

Here's how it could work: Every time the topic of adding new bunkers or planting trees comes up, ask the people in favor of these costly projects if they wouldn't rather save their money and play a ball that reverts back to, say, 1995 distances.

Many will be aghast and give you a resounding "no!" Others will say they would be open to such an idea as an alternative to a costly renovation, but that they can't envision *other* golfers going along with the idea.

"I would, but nobody else would," they'll say.

Nod and reply, "Thank you."

That's all you have to do. Plant the idea. Put it out there as an alternative to all of the grotesque ideas suggested to offset the hot ball. A distance rollback will only work when golfers begin to think that they came up with the idea.

And how, exactly, would a restricted ball work within the rules of golf? It's simpler than you might think.

A LOCAL RULE

Courses could invoke a local rule that the Classic Course Ball *may* be used. All 8 million other USGA rules would still apply. Naturally, a regular foursome will have to agree that each will use the ball in order to have a fair match, and all players in the club championship would have to use the ball if the course in question decided to embrace the idea.

What about handicaps? As we know, course ratings, slope, and handicaps are important. Courses would have to be rated based on the Classic Course Ball. This satisfies those who will rejoice when the course rating and slope go up after the local association finds that the course plays tougher with the new (old) ball. Handicaps will travel well again. All will be right with the world.

And it's all optional. The course rating for the latest version of golf can remain and be used for handicapping as well. Take your pick.

Who will make the Classic Course Ball? A shrewd company willing to take a low-risk chance. By being the first, they'll dominate the initial market and gain the notoriety they are always paying millions to secure.

This "first" manufacturer will have a patent on the ball, and someone like Augusta National Chairman Hootie Johnson might turn to them when he gets tired of rearranging his course each summer. And if they're really bright, this company will work closely with PGA of America professionals to establish the ball at *their* courses. The caveat for the pros will be the manufacturer's policy of selling the Classic Course Ball through "green grass" accounts as opposed to non-golf course vendors (accounts which hopefully still benefit the pro who owns or gets a percentage of shop sales).

Think about it. Company A introduces the Classic Course Ball, and prestigious clubs like Pine Valley or Cypress Point start selling it in their shop. Members use it in club championships or invitationals. Word gets around.

Then the ball is used in a tournament, maybe the local city amateur or a college event. Good players jump on the bandwagon, closely followed by those who *think* they're good players.

Suddenly, that ball becomes pretty cool at any course—public or private—under 7,100 yards.

What does the golf industry have to lose by giving golfers the option to make this minor correction? Participation numbers and revenue are down, and despite claims that technology makes golf more fun, it is not sustaining play and never will. Fun rounds of golf that don't take all day to play—not the dream of another 10-yard distance fix—will keep people in the sport.

MASTERS BALL?

"I would play The Masters with a Wiffle ball."

—BILLY ANDRADE

The Masters Ball scenario also makes a lot of sense. Why? For starters, the course has been changed for the worse by trying to keep up with technology. As Tom Weiskopf said, it's beginning to look like a cadaver picked at for too long by too many medical students.

More importantly, Augusta National has the authority to introduce such a ball. Company representatives and other golf big-wigs like to hang out under Augusta's big oak, and they will always want (and need) this perk. They will neither sue the Augusta National Golf Club nor have the courage to compel their staff members to sit out the Masters.

Is the Masters Ball an option the club would consider?

"If technology brings about change in the next several years like we've seen in the past several years, then we may have to consider equipment specifications for The Masters," Hootie Johnson said in 2002 before another huge distance increase in 2003, with no effective resolution in sight.

Could such a ball be made? After all, we're talking about a golf ball with the flight characteristics of circa 1995.

"While it would be an expensive proposition for us to make a golf ball for one tournament a year, it could be done," Callaway spokesman Larry Dorman told the Associated Press. "Based on talking to our top golf-ball people and our research and development people, we could maintain launch angle, spin and aerodynamics, but reduce ball speed."

In the December 2003 edition of *Golf World*, Top Flite vice president of research and development Tom Kennedy explained that players with swing speeds over 115 mph get a boost with certain balls that the average player can't get. "The transfer of energy of the club to the ball at various speeds is not linear," Kennedy said. He added that Top Flite *could* make a ball that goes a shorter distance at high swing speeds, while not changing the game for the average player.

Now try not to laugh here, but the folks at Titleist, who have out-innovated just about everyone, say it would take up to 3 years to develop such a ball!

"It's not like resizing your computer screen, or saying, 'OK, I've got a 14 font, let's go to a 10.' It's just not that simple," said Acushnet (Titleist) CEO Wally Uihlein, presumably with a straight face. "Making a golf ball is a fairly sophisticated endeavor. To ratchet down the velocity . . . will change how the ball performs. You won't have the same trajectory, spin rate, launch conditions."

And then Uihlein shared this pearl.

"I don't think they want to do that," he said, presumably referring to Augusta National. "They want to see players play the product they're pushing to the public. If you see a ball that goes short, the public doesn't want that ball. They want a ball that goes farther and can help their game."

If "they" means the folks at Augusta National, "they" have no stake in the "product" being pushed. Why would "they" care about anything except presenting an exciting and challenging Masters that is played in conditions similar to past Masters?

Former USGA President Sandy Tatum, who would prefer a distance rollback over "bifurcation," feels the situation is so far "out of control" that the introduction of a tournament ball is now an acceptable solution, even with the risks involved.

Tatum "cheered" when Hootie Johnson suggested he might issue his own ball specifications for Masters play.

"I do think that Augusta could bring it off," Tatum says. "I do have to say if that's the only way to go, then there has been an abdication of governance."

Whether it's a change in USGA testing, a tournament ball, a Masters ball, or a Wiffle ball, something needs to happen to return an emphasis on skill over pushing product to the public. And it even sounds like there is a solution that wouldn't affect the everyday golfer.

DON'T FORGET THE INFLUENCE OF MATCH PLAY

"As each year goes by I fear the true sporting spirit of match play is less and less in evidence. We find a growing disposition for play to concentrate on the figures that are registered at a hole rather than on the question of whether the hole is lost or won in a purely friendly match."

—TOM SIMPSON, GOLF ARCHITECT

Even though match play is still used for most friendly (and some not so friendly) everyday rounds, the format is typically cited by modern professionals as a lesser version of golf, one that is not as "pure" as stroke play.

A recent article in *Golf World* compared the NCAA Championship to the U.S. Amateur, and gave the edge to the NCAA as the better event because it's a stroke-play tournament. At match play, fluky things happen.

One college coach cited the 2002 amateur final (when Ricky Barnes edged Hunter Mahan) as irrefutable proof that the NCAA format was better. The coach implied that Barnes was more erratic during the match.

Am I missing something? Is this a beauty contest or a hole-by-hole format that determines who gets the ball in the hole first the most times?

In a match, the players play against each other on the same course under the same conditions. In the NCAA stroke play, a player who tees off at 8 A.M. in approaching clouds might have a monumental advantage over someone teeing off at 12:30 P.M. in a windy downpour.

Yet, match play is considered to be more prone to fluke events, while stroke play is a more reliable method of determining a champion. Match play is used in everyday golf more than any other format. It's the reason we have the handicap system, even though handicaps are based on aggregate scores instead of hole-by-hole tallies (which may explain why the handicap system has its doubters—more on that later).

Still, match play is fun and certainly fair. It allows players of all levels to have a friendly competition. And, the Ryder Cup is easily the most compelling event in golf because of the varied formats played under the match play "umbrella."

So why is match play dying in professional golf, and why should this matter for everyday golf?

Network television does not like match play. Even though it is far more compelling when a match is close, especially if played on an interesting course, match play is just too unpredictable for the cameras. It's too tough to figure out when and where the match will end, and there's too much dead air time between shots. There are just too many toos.

Professional golfers argue that match play allows "chance" to enter the golfing equation. (And stroke play doesn't, when played on a course with freak pin placements, super narrow fairways, and goofy architecture?)

In an age when we try to level the playing field for all and protect everyone's individual rights, there apparently isn't room for a format that rewards skill, thought, courage, well-timed aggressiveness, and hard work.

But here's the kicker: Many of the greatest golf courses were designed with match play in mind because that was the primary format in use when the classics were built.

Most of the so-called masterpieces of today were designed with stroke play in mind.

What is the difference?

The classic courses were crafted without fear that golfers would cry foul over a quirky design feature that might interrupt an otherwise excellent day of pars and birdies. Golfers did not expect every green to hold a direct aerial approach shot. In a match play setting, all players have to deal with the same feature, and par is not of any great significance.

Today, par is everything, with a handicap system built around it. Modern holes are all-too-often designed to fit a par of 3, 4, or 5. In the old days, holes were designed first to take advantage of natural features or to create the opportunity for interesting golf. A par was affixed to the hole at a later time, based on what was created.

The best holes in golf usually fudge the definition of par. The great short par 4s are really par 3½s. The same goes for the most dramatic par 5s. They seem a little easier than a par of exactly 5. The revered long par 4s and long par 3s push the extremes of their par, often playing as short par 5s and short 4s. By extending the boundaries of par, the holes impose interesting match-play situations while failing under the spotlight of stroke play where those par figures have to be more precise.

But golf will never be fair, whether the format is stroke or match play.

HANDICAPPED BY HANDICAPPING

"Our present method of averaging scores to attain a handicap has been working from a Whole to arrive at a standard for the Parts, instead of intelligently working from the Parts to determine the efficiency of the Whole."

—MAX BEHR

The present-day handicapping system calls for all eighteen-hole scores to be turned in, reinforcing the eighteen-hole stroke play mentality over match play (or just a leisurely day on the links). The stroke-play grind places the importance on fairness and equity above design features that, if allowed, would make hole-by-hole matches more fun, but scorecards more messy.

If individual hole posting—the "parts" as Max Behr put it—was used instead of an eighteen-hole number to calculate handicaps, it would not matter how many holes a golfer played, or even how many holes a course had. Such a system would more accurately reflect how golfers fared on individual holes, thus allowing a computer to figure out a more honest handicap than the eighteen-hole total does. Courses would also have more accurate handicap designations for individual holes based on computer breakdowns of past player performance.

With hole-by-hole posting, it wouldn't matter if a golfer had played one hole fifty times and another golfer had played it ten times—the computer could analyze their performances and create a handicap the same way it now does for the eighteen-hole scheme.

Apparently the ability to compute handicaps on this basis is already in the USGA's Golf Handicap and Information Network (GHIN) system. One objection has been that posting the "parts" instead of the "whole" would be more time consuming: Many golfers wouldn't turn in scores if they had to enter all the "parts" to the round.

HANDICAPS ARE NOT GOING DOWN . . .
SO WHY SHOULD WE REGULATE?

Another strange argument from Far Hills to justify the USGA's failure to regulate equipment has appeared in several articles, including this one from a July 2004 article in the *Contra Costa Times*.

The tale goes like this: The United States Golf Association has been tracking handicap indexes since 1991, when the average handicap indexes were 16.3 for men and 29.7 for women. In 2003, the averages were 15.2 for men and 27.9 for women.

"You can see it's not like everyone's going down some tremendous value," said Kevin O'Connor, senior director of handicapping and information services for the USGA. "So the quote 'purchase of a golf game' hasn't necessarily resulted in a significant change in everyone's handicaps. We still struggle out there."

But the follow-up comment is never made: Equipment isn't making the game significantly easier for those who are most avid. Yet, the USGA agrees with equipment manufacturers who say the game will grow only if there is less regulation, allowing the companies to get more of the latest (supposedly easier to use) equipment in the hands of golfers.

If the latest equipment is not lowering handicaps of avid golfers who are more likely to benefit, how will such equipment help the beginner?

But with a user-friendly computer program, golfers could enter hole-by-hole scores in less than a minute.

Besides giving a more accurate reflection of one's ability, the big-picture ramifications would be significant for the sport.

Architects are often asked to consider how the "slope" or the "course rating" will be affected by specific design features. Restoration specialists are told not to alter certain features because they could make the

---

course's slope higher than necessary. In other cases architects are asked to add new hazards to increase the course rating while not affecting the slope!

It's akin to telling an artist what colors and what size canvas she has to use based on the interior lighting and wall space planned for the painting, regardless of her ideas or the subject matter.

Golf has lost a certain amount of character because architecture is currently shaped around the needs of stroke play and the handicap system. Course design should offer an exciting challenge for the player to overcome. Satisfaction comes from overcoming challenges successfully. Posting scores and maintaining a handicap are important, but secondary to the pleasures of playing.

Because of the eighteen-hole stroke-play format, architects often don't even consider provocative design elements that would provide everyday golfers with genuine satisfaction, excitement, and fond golfing memories.

THEME COURSES: KITSCH OR FUN?

GOLFING VERSIONS OF DISNEYLAND AT
LEAST PRESENT ENTICING GOLF HOLES

The wave of new theme courses means which of the following? That (A) the game has taken tasteless, tacky, and embarrassing to a new low, or (B) there is a wonderful irony in this fast-growing segment of the golf development business.

No matter what you think of the Disneyfication of American golf, the concept of celebrating and replicating classic design holes and bunkers has allowed architects to present something they are often prevented from trying in a new design: interesting, quirky, exciting holes to play.

Sure, sometimes these amusement-park replicas fail to remind anyone of the original; and yes, the "Masters" scoreboards are way over the top for those Amen Corner reproductions. But deep bunkers, blind shots, option holes, and many of the other oddities that lent interest to "traditional" classic courses are returning via theme courses.

One of the golf's mysteries is how players can travel to a noted course, enjoy the oddities of its design, and then return and label the same features on their home course as "unfair." If a blind shot or a treeless links-style course is presented as a theme design inspired by one of golf's hallowed grounds, the architecture is fun. But if a designer presents the same ideas as part of his own design, the client inevitably will protest, "You can't do that in modern golf!"

As the golf business suffers the consequences of building ordinary, overpriced, unsatisfying designs where repeat business is nonexistent, theme courses are emerging as a surefire way to market a course and maintain a steady stream of customers. The early examples are working because marketing comes easier, and golfers will try anything once. But theme courses experience repeat business largely because golfers have discovered the joy of playing interesting holes.

One can only hope that the themes we see in the coming years are a bit more subtle, shedding some of the kitsch. A concept course such as architect George Bahto's Stonebridge (New York), took an ordinary, home-lined site and transformed it into a must-see course because of Bahto's fascinating green complex designs. And there is architect Brian Silva's Black Creek, where Seth Raynor's style was respectfully borrowed or adopted to create a golf course that is provoking enthusiastic discussion because of its interesting and at times original architecture.

The theme element merely allowed Bahto and Silva to present design ideas that, in today's market, would not be acceptable under the auspices of a contemporary George Bahto or Brian Silva design.

"I think many parts of most new courses have—or perhaps I should say, should have themes," says Silva. "They should be based on classic characteristics and classic golf holes. Now whether or not you, as an architect, decide to directly lift the 'look' along with the lifted characteristic or strategy, is the next question."

Let's hope the lifting and borrowing become more subtle—so understated that the theme or replica labels eventually fade away, and talented architects are given the freedom to present their own interesting designs. But until that day, theme courses at least present designs that golfers can discuss and enjoy, attributes that the golf business needs to take more seriously.

A THINK TANK . . . THAT THINKS

". . . it is safe to say that no game in the whole realm of sport has been so mis-written and unwritten as golf. This is very strange, for probably there is no other game that is so canvassed and discussed by its followers. The reason may possibly be found in the fact that golfers are a most conservative class of people, and that they follow wonderfully the line of thought laid down for them by others. This at its best is uninteresting; at its worst most pernicious."
—P. A. VAILLE, 1912

Northern California–based architect Tom Johnson emailed me to ask why golf does not have its own "think tank." Good question.

Think tanks are government- or business-sponsored groups that research, brainstorm, and look ahead.

Golf has no shortage of cocktail congregations. They end up as an excuse for a vacation followed by a press release announcing a new feel-good, corporatesque initiative. When these execs do meet and talk specifics, they share tips on protecting their anti-trust exemptions and nonprofit tax shelters, and that's about it.

Somehow golf's worst over-spenders and pillagers are always invited to these affairs, as are a few bottom-line executive types who complain that Wall Street is hounding them because no one is growing the game, making it hard for them to report better third-quarter earnings than last year.

So why is there no "think tank" composed of creative folks who sit behind closed doors brainstorming ways to improve the sport?

Golf is a conservative pastime by nature and typically leery of new ideas. Think tanks have been known to come up with some strange, if not downright goofy, schemes.

You might have heard of DARPA. That's the Defense Advanced Research Projects Agency. Over the years, DARPA helped create the Internet, GPS systems, the computer mouse, and stealth technology.

Birdies.

In 2003, DARPA came up with a crackpot scheme to improve our foreign intelligence with an online futures' market where folks tucked away as far as the mountains of Pakistan could place online bets, wagering where the next terrorist might strike.

Triple bogey.

It wouldn't take long for an effective golf think tank to point out how unimaginative and tedious the PGA Tour has become, and how a more entertaining tour could reinvigorate recreational golf.

The think tank might ask why it costs so much to build a USGA green and they'd point out that the USGA's GHIN handicap system tends to create all sorts of unintended golfing side effects like the stroke-play mentality, the stigma attached to nine-hole rounds, and the silly emphasis on course ratings instead of fun.

And, a think tank would point out that golf should be a steadily thriving community sport, with an ancient model in Scotland and a modern example in Sweden.

The golf industry needs some imaginative thinking to inject life into the recreational game. Golf must improve its image environmentally, explain the long-term impact of the distance issue to golfers, and find ways to share innovative ideas that give developers incentives to create fun and affordable golf facilities.

Here are some suggested guidelines for a think tank:

• No organizational blazers should be allowed in meetings.

• Seats will *not* be reserved for those with an interest in covering their rear ends.

• No holders of golf-industry stocks will be eligible.

• Anyone who suggests that all the golf industry needs is a fresh marketing campaign can save their breath.

• The think tank will not listen to architects who build $25 million golf courses and brag about how much they spent. Those who help them run up such tabs also need not apply.

• Superintendents who've done wonders on a $400,000 budget will be consulted for suggestions. Those who grumble that $1 million doesn't go as far as it used to should not be invited.

• Golf professionals who have schmoozed their way to the top can stay home. We only want those who have developed creative programs that make golf more fun to take up.

• No one listed in *Golf Digest*'s annual "power" rankings will be invited.

• And finally, a golf think tank should assemble those who generate ideas that build on golf's greatest traditions while thinking of ways to grow the sport based on the principles of affordability and fun.

REVAMP THE USGA
EXECUTIVE COMMITTEE

"I've always been a big supporter of the USGA, but not anymore. The sad part is they've lost credibility, not so much with the mainstream players, but with the true amateurs and tournament players who care so much about the game."
— BARRY VAN GERBIG, PRESIDENT OF SEMINOLE, JANUARY 2004

"Discussion in America means dissent."
— JAMES THURBER

The USGA is worth salvaging, but not in its current configuration. The organization has a paid staff, yet decision-making is handled by the all-volunteer executive committee that has drifted from its mission and listens to the staff only at select times. Worse, the committee consists of too many like-minded people reaffirming too much ignorance.

The USGA executive committee used to tolerate dissent, but a long list of recent members who found themselves suddenly "voted off the island" reveals the presence of what our military might call a form of "incestuous amplification." In other words, it has become a group of people of similar backgrounds and thought processes who talk only to one another and validate their mutually held views. And the more sure they become, the more fearful others become of dissenting, so they fill committee positions with even more like-minded folks.

Had dissent within the USGA been tolerated, folks like Win Padgett (who voiced concern over dropping *Golf Journal*), John Vardaman (who supported equipment regulation), and Carole Semple Thompson (who spoke up about the need to upgrade Golf House) might have lasted a little longer. Several former presidents and committee higher-ups are no longer consulted because they have voiced dissenting views.

One former executive committee member who is physically handicapped joined the expanding cadre of former USGAers because he complained that Golf House was not in compliance with the Americans with Disabilities Act code while it was cozying up to pro golfer Casey Martin after he qualified for the 1998 U.S. Open.

The executive director is paid lavishly to guide the volunteers, and under David Fay's reign the organization has seemingly lacked the strong, consistent voice that it sorely needs.

More importantly, the USGA and other golf organizations need to accept dissenting views if they hope to better anticipate future issues. Because a strong and credible USGA can only be a good thing for golf.

Aware they had problems, the USGA took some action in 2004. What did they do? They blamed the past presidents!

A small group of former USGA presidents who have been pushing for a rollback in equipment were pretty much accused of being at fault for all that is wrong in the world by the current executive committee leadership.

Most media accounts of the USGA's 2004 winter meeting bought into the notion that the past presidents were to blame for the USGA's inability to do much of anything right these days.

Inexplicably demonized in the whole process was Frank "Sandy" Tatum, widely regarded as the most prominent and important past president whose track record wreaks of devotion to the game. Tatum and other past presidents were portrayed in Golfweek and Golf World as having lost touch with the game, and therefore were no longer qualified to select who should be running the USGA. Not only was the charge inaccurate, but it also demonstrated how low the current USGA leadership was willing to go shift blame.

The executive committee nomination process has always been murky. No one has fully understood how executive committee members are selected, or how certain members were chosen over seemingly more qualified folks. And because so few non-country-club golfers have made it to the committee, the USGA has always produced the occasional committee member who is out of touch with the everyday game.

The new nomination process really won't change the fact that the organization appears to be mired in a group-think–driven approach, determined to ignore its mistakes while forging ahead with various self-interests. In fact, the new procedures may expedite the process of signing up like-minded thinkers.

Under the new system that will determine the 2006 nominations, past presidents will lose their autonomous control and be replaced by a new committee that includes the sitting USGA president, a recent past president, and individuals from USGA member clubs.

Golf World's Ron Sirak wrote of the new nominating process, "This may seem like a matter far removed from the average golfer, but it is an issue that strikes at the heart of the game. It's all about what kind of clubs you can have in your bag and what kind of ball you can hit with them. Make no mistake about it: This was a victory for the equipment industry."

BRING BACK THE STYMIE
(OCCASIONALLY, ANYWAY)

THE MOST COMPELLING FORMAT HAS ELUDED
TELEVISED GOLF FOR SOME MYSTERIOUS REASON

"I have never experienced so many chills and thrills in so short a time."
—BOBBY JONES, REFERRING TO A STYMIE SITUATION

Few golfers realize that the greatest debate in golf history was not over square grooves, springlike effects, or the golf ball. It was over the "stymie." And it raged for nearly 50 years!

Before 1952, when the stymie was completely eliminated from golf, balls could *not* be marked and picked up on the green in order to allow your opponent an unobstructed line to the hole. But before you decide you were born in the right decade and applaud this hard-won rule change, consider Bobby Jones's 1959 essay on the subject from his biography, *Golf Is My Game*.

In Chapter 18, "The Stymie—Let's Have It Back," Jones explained in detail how the stymie worked and gave rather convincing evidence about its positive effect on *match* play. Jones wrote:

> With the stymie in the game, match-play golf becomes an exciting duel in which the player must always be on guard against a sudden, often demoralizing thrust. More than anything else, it points up the value of always being the closer to the hole on the shot to the green and after the first putt. The player who can maintain the upper hand in the play up to the hole rarely suffers from a stymie.
>
> In my observation, the stymie has more often been the means of enforcing the decision in favor of the deserving player, rather than the contrary.

I think it merits a respected place in the game. I know a return to it would greatly enhance the interest and excitement of match play golf for player and spectator alike.

Jones was not a rabble-rouser who stirred things up just to get attention. His experience as a tournament contestant and sportsman told him that the stymie added one more dimension to this once multidimensional sport.

Perhaps the stymie could come back occasionally to spice up some local match-play tournaments, or perhaps in a "silly-season" match-play event on the PGA, LPGA, or Senior PGA Tour? A little excitement wouldn't hurt golf, would it?

RETURN THE CADDIE, SCRAP THE FIRST TEES

"I always push hard with developers for caddie programs, and particularly for using youngsters during the summer months, giving them the opportunity to make some money, to learn the game, and to absorb important lessons about life by being around intelligent, successful adults."

—JACK NICKLAUS

One particularly sad casualty of our market-obsessed society is the caddie, and in particular, the young caddie.

We all know the reason why caddying is gone from golf. Caddies eat into cart revenue.

While some clubs and a few upscale public courses still have them, caddies are nearly extinct in the United States. Where caddies are still allowed, they often must be over 18, so you rarely find them to be young men and women even though the word caddie is derived from the French word "cadet," meaning young boy.

In the good old days when people took themselves a little less seriously and enjoyed walking, commercial interests weren't driving the sport. So, kids and young adults would carry your clubs for a small fee. They could make decent money caddying over the summer months. Byron Nelson and Ben Hogan both fell in love with the game while caddying as young boys at Glen Garden Country Club in Texas. Both referred to those days as their inspiration to pursue a career in golf. Many baby boomers who play golf today got into golf through caddying.

That indirect, subtle way to learn the intricacies of the game is much different than attending a class run by a paid instructor who lectures the kids about the rules, etiquette, and how to hold a club. You can guess which is a better way to learn.

THE EVANS SCHOLARSHIP

The Western Golf Association administers the largest privately funded college scholarship program in the nation. Since 1930, when the first two Evans Scholars enrolled at Northwestern University, more than 7,600 outstanding young men and women have participated in the program, named after golfing great Chick Evans.

Each year more than 800 deserving caddies attend college on a full tuition and housing grant awarded by the Evans Scholars Foundation. Caddies must be nominated by their club and meet four requirements to qualify: they must rank among the top 25 percent of their high school class, have a superior caddie record for two or more years, show financial need, and have outstanding personal character.

More than 200 new scholars are chosen annually after an applicant's interview with a scholarship committee. Almost all Evans Scholars attend one of the fourteen universities where the foundation maintains a Chapter House and the program is the largest scholarship organization in sports (*www.evans-scholarsfoundation.com*).

The following golf associations participate in the program and should be commended for their efforts:

For the golfer, there is nothing more enjoyable than having your clubs carried by a quiet but devoted caddie.

Instead of trying to return caddying to golf as a way to introduce new players and secure the future, the higher powers have tried to create feel-good, inherently limited youth programs like the First Tee that serve as nice window dressing and perfect tax write-offs for large corporations. Sure, they offer instruction and facilities to start, but that's about where it ends.

Arizona Golf Association
Buffalo District Golf Association
Chicago District Golf Association
Colorado Golf Association
Golf Association of Michigan
Greater Cincinnati Golf Association
Illinois Women's Golf Association
Indiana Golf Association
Kansas City Golf Association
Kentucky Golf Association
Minnesota Golf Association
Northeastern Wisconsin Golf Association
Northern California Golf Association
Ohio Golf Association
Oregon Golf Association
South Dakota Golf Association
St. Louis District Golf Association
Syracuse District Golf Association
Toledo District Golf Association
Washington State Golf Association
Western Pennsylvania Golf Association
Wisconsin State Golf Association

The real joy of becoming a golfer is learning the game's lore, experiencing the fun of competing and the challenge of trying to improve. Caddying provides the perfect first step and initial exposure to the elements of golf that can't be taught in a classroom. The First Tee does provide a start, but where are the affordable and interesting courses that graduates can move up to after getting hooked?

Caddying can be a lucrative summer job, and through the Evans Scholarship program (more on this later), can even pay someone's way through college. And as we all know from the film *Caddyshack*, it can

---

WESTCHESTER GOLF ASSOCIATION
DOING ITS PART

According to an August 2004 *New York Times* story, a comprehensive caddie training program headed by the Westchester Golf Association is helping return the caddie to New York–area clubs. The association coordinates caddie programs in 82 clubs in and around Westchester, with 295 students receiving money through its caddie scholarship fund.

In April, the association holds a caddie academy, offering instructional films, books, on-course training, and a certification process for budding caddies.

According to the *Times*, "Caddies usually make more than $100 for essentially a half-day's work. Most clubs set a flat caddying fee per round, but the real pay comes from tips. Most caddies say they earn an average of about $120 total for carrying two bags eighteen holes. It can be a bit less, or much more if the players are high rollers playing for serious money . . . fringe benefits often include playing privileges on Mondays (when most clubs are closed), college scholarships and the opportunity to meet influential members who might come in handy in future job searches."

---

be fun to have a laugh at the expense of older, more serious golfers who make fools of themselves on the golf course. (Think Judge Smails.)

For every character they meet caddying, they also are introduced to plenty of intelligent, successful people who might just open doors to these kids if a life in golf doesn't work out.

If golf is going to be a sport for the masses or even if it hopes to have a healthy future, our lawyers and course operators need to find a way to let kids get involved casually and on their own terms. Shoot, if you need to take a $10 "cart preservation fee" from the caddies, they'll still make good money.

At the very least, courses need to let kids join their parents as spectators out on the course, something that is often forbidden because of liability concerns. Or, heaven forbid, the young golfer might try a shot or two without paying a green fee!

Whether they stay with the sport or not, caddying makes young people better adults because of their experiences watching elders play golf and observing etiquette and human interaction. Caddying helps kids build self-esteem in a natural manner, not in a forced, feel-good five-point program.

And remember how much it means for a child to feel included by adults? Imagine how rewarding it is for a young person when an adult actually asks for advice, even if it's just a decision between a five- or a six-iron.

Ben Hogan and Byron Nelson found sponsors through their caddying experience, and some clubs, such as Caves Valley Golf Club in Maryland, encourage their caddies and members to interact with the hope of helping their caddies move up in the business world. Several have taken prestigious jobs with these members.

Let's find a way to introduce kids to golf through caddying. It'll grow the game, which is good for everyone, even for the course operators who don't like the dent caddies make in their cart revenues.

Oh, and it wouldn't hurt people to do a little more walking, either.

RESTORE CLASSIC MUNI'S

"The mother art is architecture. Without an architecture of our own we have no soul of our own civilization."

—Frank Lloyd Wright

Why can't there be more Bethpage Blacks? Since 1996, when the "restoration" of the Black Course project was announced, the golf industry and USGA considered this a one-time project. The 2002 U.S. Open revenues would fund the course reconstruction and maintenance overhaul. The lure of an Open was the only way the USGA could dictate to the state bureaucracy what had to be done. An Open bid and a lecture from executive director David Fay about free publicity was the only way to get Rees Jones to donate his services and to attract some of the maintenance industry's top young and willing-to-work-long-hours talent.

However, as the new course construction boom ends, architects, shapers, and other construction experts are looking for work. Existing golf course budgets are shrinking, meaning that talented assistant superintendents and experienced maintenance personnel are available. In other words, good help is eager to please at prices that make restoring public courses financially viable.

But are the parks and recreation districts willing to tackle projects for the good of the game and their customers without the lure of a major tournament?

Former USGA president Sandy Tatum might tell you the answer is no. After years of struggling to get the City of San Francisco to understand the rewards of a full-scale renovation at Harding Park, a $16 million redo of Harding is complete with the PGA Tour likely bringing tournaments there.

A noble project, but $16 million is a hefty price—eight times the cost of what a subtle restoration could accomplish to rejuvenate a rundown classic.

The list of publicly owned courses designed by legendary architects is long and covers most of America. But their architecture has been compromised. In some cases the deterioration is typical of an old course, in others the original layout has been corrupted by "renovations," and more extensive work is needed.

It would cost as much as $5 million to undo years of foolish alterations on some courses, while many more just need an inexpensive bunker restoration, newly grassed tees, enlarged greens, and an overall maintenance upgrade. If restorations are managed by available experts in the design, construction, and maintenance field with contractors kept in line, such projects can be carried out at a price that would neither require a major championship to justify nor require a hike in green fees to pay for.

However, a few big-name architects are currently seeking "Bethpage-like" projects because they want to boost their image. A few management companies and architects are trying to do similar projects, but their motivations are suspect.

This is not who we want and who we can afford to do these projects. Yes, it's cool to have them there for opening day, with the bigwigs having their pictures taken with celebrities, but this is not the way to do things economically or sensibly.

If there's an old layout designed by one of the game's great architects, say Colt and Alison's Timber Point on Long Island or A. W. Tillinghast's Cedar Crest in Dallas, the easiest way to spark renewed interest in the game or to retain longtime golfers is to breathe life into these neglected classics. Governments protect and restore historic buildings at much greater costs. Why not golf courses?

Upgrading classic municipal courses without requiring significant fee hikes would serve as a legitimate use of public money because the golf courses are actually used and supported by taxpayers. And if managed halfway decently, they make the money back.

The expected wave of soon-to-be First Tee program graduates means there will be future taxpayers using these public gems. Restoring the best design elements of courses like Chandler Egan's North Fulton in Atlanta, Hugh Wilson's Cobbs Creek in Philadelphia, or George Thomas's Griffith Park in Los Angeles would give First Tee grads quality architecture on which to take their game to the next level, something the First Tee program currently doesn't offer.

And unless the youngsters have a chance to experience thought-provoking design elements, they are unlikely to reach their potential—or even continue to play golf.

As we saw at Bethpage, interesting architecture breeds enthusiasm that benefits all golfers. We commonly see aging shopping districts rejuvenated or new baseball parks built to resemble old ones. These places exude charm while restoring a sense of community and excitement even for the most jaded.

The same should happen with classic public golf courses.

GO NATIVE

USING NATIVE PLANTS AND GRASSES TO SAVE
WATER AND RESTORE A "SENSE OF PLACE"

"Only as far as the masters of the world have called in nature to their aid, can they reach the height of magnificence."

—RALPH WALDO EMERSON

Not long ago most Americans didn't pay much attention to food certified "organic" by strict United States Department of Agriculture (USDA) guidelines. But now that more people are aware that an "organic" label means they are likely to be supporting local farmers and eating more wholesome, non-industrialized food, the movement has taken hold. Large food-product corporations are even trying to jump on the organic bandwagon.

The "native" plant movement took on a similar connotation for most Americans: sounds nice, but what does it really mean financially or aesthetically to use native plants in your landscaping?

A sure sign that incorporating natives improves the bottom line and creates a more conscientious image is when big companies jump on the bandwagon. You may have noticed business parks have been converting their landscaping to native. You can almost guarantee the movement is here to stay.

What do these revolutions mean to the golf industry?

Some would say nothing, but plenty of superintendents, architects, and even a few golfers feel it's time for the industry to say to the nongolfing world that golf embraces native looks and will consider all practical means to use less water.

WHAT DOES NATIVE REALLY MEAN?

na·tive—Originating, growing, or produced in a certain place or region; indigenous.

Once established, native re-vegetation in the form of plant material, wildflowers, and prairie grasses sustains wildlife, requires less water and less care, and looks healthy year-round with occasional bursts of color.

Slowly, sometimes reluctantly, a native golf movement has begun with developments like the Golf Course Superintendents Association of America's push for courses to give an acre back to nature or Audubon International's environmentally friendly certification program. However, the native golf trend will only expand into a revolution if golfers can be sold on the benefits to their local environment—and their pocketbooks.

With rising costs and water privatization looming (or already a deregulated disaster in some cities), golf courses must find ways to reduce water use. It is *the* essential issue for the golf industry. Converting out-of-play areas, grassy hazards, and clubhouse landscaping can make a difference.

SELLING NATIVE

"There is great charm and beauty in the varying shades of color on a golf course."

—ALISTER MACKENZIE

After the "rounds played" slowdown in 2003, the golf industry should be open to short-term investments that reduce long-term water and maintenance costs. We've heard the warnings about water usage but as many have already found out, breaking away from the modern American golf aesthetic will not be an easy sell.

The average American golfer wants a golf course to be part Disneyland (vibrant, but sanitized), part cemetery (no lost balls), part corporate statement (we're in control of our landscape), and part game board (precisely defined fairways and roughs). Golfers also expect their courses to be lauded as a masterpiece unique to the world of golf, even if it looks just like five other courses in the neighborhood.

The greatest designs in the world tend to avoid the characteristics that most golfers want in their home course. These epic layouts have vaulted their way to the top of rankings in spite of their close ties to a native, sometimes rugged environment.

By my count, fourteen of *Golf Magazine*'s 2003 top twenty courses in the world could be classified as "native courses." They reflect a sense of place by playing through indigenous landscaping. Many are highlighted by native shrubbery accenting bunkers or neighboring prairie grasses. These world-renowned courses do not intentionally landscape with non-native trees, plants, or prairie grasses.

A case could be made for others in the top twenty trying to soften some of their man-made edges. At Pebble Beach, efforts have been made in recent years to restore native grass areas and a more rugged, indigenous look to the bunkers. Non-native and horribly invasive ice plant has been eradicated.

Native giants like Pine Valley, Cypress Point, Shinnecock Hills, Royal Melbourne, Pinehurst, Sand Hills, Pacific Dunes, and every Scottish links have become unique commodities because they incorporate native plant materials and grasses to help define their aesthetic character. Golfers will travel long distances to experience these one-of-a-kind settings.

Sure, the holes would still be fun to play without the color and texture provided by indigenous plant material. But these designs are elevated to supreme status because they look like nothing else in the world. The smells, sights, and even the sounds prove unforgettable thanks to the home-grown environment and the absence of intrusive, non-native touches.

Pointing to the best courses in the world may be the strongest selling point for those hoping to return out-of-play areas, grassy hazards, clubhouse landscaping, and other portions of a course to native plant material.

Every region of the United States has its own unique native flavor, and golf has ignored this in favor of imported looks that are not inherent to the local environment. Or more often, during the construction process all existing plants were clumsily plowed away, with the constructors arrogantly insisting on starting over with costly relandscaping. This expense is passed down to the customers.

Golf's environmental hubris has led to an extreme economic impact, with increased water usage and expensive maintenance required to sustain areas that could have just as easily been left alone or cared for in a limited way.

Only recently have architects and superintendents become more understanding of the backlash from environmentalists, many of whom view golf courses as chemical waste dumps—not because of any substantial data telling them so, but simply based on the aesthetics of golf. Even those who wouldn't call themselves hardcore environmentalists will point to wall-to-wall green grass, pin-striped mowing patterns, blinding white sand, offset by a fountain-adorned lake as just a little obnoxious.

The most extreme words we hear describing golf include "garish," "excessive," and anything else that conjures up images of disproportionate water and chemical use. Sometimes the outsider views are reasonable; most times they are baseless—except when it comes to modern golf aesthetics—because golf can do better.

No, a course can never look as natural as a meadow or a genuine native prairie, but a little effort can take some of the edge off and earn your course more acceptance in the community.

Unaccountably, some golfers take pride in the way their courses stick out like a sore thumb. They *like* the front lawn, cemetery-esque look of a golf course that appears to dominate its environment.

At the same time, golfers don't like paying more for water, and they wonder why their course isn't recognized in the rankings. (The thought never crosses their mind that the added expense and sterilized setting creates an experience too similar to other courses.)

Don't hesitate to point to the magazine lists and suggest that the best courses in the world attract people from all over because their environmental experience is unique. Clip magazine photographs and put them in an album. Do anything you can to show that the revered designs weave their way along and through a native setting you won't find anywhere else.

If that doesn't work, there's always the economic alternative. Tell 'em how much all that extra water, fertilizer, and pesticide costs.

SAVING WATER

Austin's Lost Creek Golf Club sits on Barton Creek in Texas's capital city. Operated by Club Corporation of America, the 1972 Terry Dill design (since redesigned by Jeff Brauer) joined forces with the Lady Bird Johnson Wildflower Center to return several acres to native wildflowers.

The Austin Watershed Protection Agency has created buffer zones along the creek, and the club has accepted the agency's demand for a native buffer and set an example for all of golf.

A self-described "native nut," superintendent Steve Houser has seen golf architects take "existing properties and go backwards with them." Lost Creek was not unlike many other Texas courses. Solid and certainly providing playing pleasure, it lacked color and texture.

Under Houser's supervision, the club started a 3-year plan to create the required buffer zone along Barton Creek while expanding the mandated 75-foot zone to 300 feet, with plans to eventually convert 11 acres to wildflowers, grasses, and native trees.

"If you add up the labor hours, water, and fertilizer spent on areas that are essentially out of play, it's crazy," says Houser.

Houser estimates that instead of using 30,000 gallons of water a week devoted to irrigate roughs in the areas now (or soon to be) converted to natives, Lost Creek will use 2,500 gallons a week to establish the areas, but soon after Houser says, "you let it go."

Heather Venhaus of the Lady Bird Johnson Wildflower Center worked with Houser and club officials on the Lost Creek project, the first for the Austin-based nonprofit organization, which is the lead voice for the North American native plant movement.

"We were very comfortable with Steve and Lost Creek and we see this as a new audience," said Venhaus. "Since golf is very popular, those people who are playing may or may not come in contact with natives and we saw this as an educational tool."

Lost Creek project leaders say inviting course officials to see the native setting was key to selling the concept. Venhaus and Houser urge other course officials to do the same if they hope to sell golfers on native conversion.

"We talked about how meadows look when they are a year old and 2 years old, and started to educate them on how natives work," says Venhaus. "Plus, we were learning how golf works."

FEEL AND PATIENCE REQUIRED

"The prairie has a beauty of its own and we should recognize and accentuate this natural beauty, its quiet level."

—FRANK LLOYD WRIGHT

A deft touch is necessary when implementing native re-vegetation. Too often, the landscape-architecture approach is used: Plants are located in straight lines; coordinating color schemes look a little too harmonized; or hydro-seeded areas have so many varieties mixed in that the effect is dizzyingly unnatural (and when fully grown, your basic automatic-lost-ball area).

Nature works in a more random and subtle manner. Tours of local botanical gardens or native plant society–recommended sites will help sell a native revegetation program. The quality of many indigenous plants surprises those who are new to the native movement.

Still, some natives don't "take." And the seasons for establishing various plants or grasses vary, so outside consultation with nurseries and native plant experts is recommended.

"We see this as an avenue to broaden golf's horizons," says Steve Houser of Lost Creek's effort. "Plus anytime we can do something to relieve some of that stress we're under—you have to take the opportunity."

Golf is certainly going to be under stress for the next few years if predictions about water availability and prices come true, which is why now is the time to relieve some of the burden through native revegetation.

THE ART THAT IS LIFE

ARTS AND CRAFTS GOLF

"Simplicity, individuality and dignity of effort."
—GUSTAV STICKLEY, ON THE PRINCIPLES DRIVING
THE ARTS AND CRAFTS MOVEMENT

Convinced that industrialization caused the degradation of work and the destruction of the environment, the Arts and Crafts cultural movement of the late nineteenth and early twentieth centuries emphasized simpler but still charming architecture. Determined to right social ills, the Arts and Crafts reformers chose art as their medium, and in particular, the hand-crafted design of homes, furniture, and gardens. The idea was to restore pride through satisfying labor, which is why the movement became known as "the art that is life."

The Arts and Crafts movement inspired much of architect Frank Lloyd Wright's design style, though he deviated in one major way. Wright believed in taking advantage of technology and machinery as long as it was "under the architect's creative control."

Golf course architects, superintendents, and their crews know the kind of satisfaction achieved through craftsmanship, on-the-job creativity, and hand labor, but they still take advantage of the latest technology. Others in the golf course industry understand the satisfaction one can derive from a job when creativity and intuition drives labor. Technology is merely one part of the equation that leads to a well-maintained golf course.

It's not a coincidence that many of the greatest golf courses were designed during the 1920s when the Arts and Crafts movement was changing the way America looked at itself. Nor is it a coincidence that

Arts and Crafts ideals are enjoying a renaissance today for many of the same reasons that initiated the movement during the late 1800s. Contemporary golf has drifted from the ideals set forth during the Arts and Crafts movement. Technology has become more important than craftsmanship.

In the early days, golf clubs were just tools for creating shots and expressing our imagination and skill. There was an art to making clubs, and many of the game's great players made their own.

Now it's the golf club's job to do the hard work, like achieving distance and accuracy and consistency. Our job is merely to refine a repeating swing that matches launch conditions in order to achieve the best results (with clubs ironed out by laborers in Mexico and Asia).

Even the most fervent admirer of technology can't deny the joys of a curving shot, a devilish pitch, or a heroic recovery play. The rush from pulling off such shots sustains golf in our hearts and minds. There is little dignity of effort in merely bashing away at the ball with a titanium, computer-matched, high-tech weapon.

John Ruskin, an Oxford University professor and one of the first to explain Arts and Crafts ideals, believed that building designers of his era had become anonymous laborers. Only by returning to more handwork would character be restored to architecture and the arts. The qualities of asymmetry, irregularity, roughness, and naturalness—the same qualities that give classic golf courses such a distinct look—were the qualities Ruskin felt drove the Arts and Crafts movement to its popular status. Such qualities were not acquired by machine, but instead required creativity and craftsmanship from those doing the design and labor.

No, golf should not be laborious, but creativity and craftsmanship are more likely to create fun than a long and straight driving contest would.

The classic golf course restoration rage is clearly an offshoot of the return to the Arts and Crafts ideals of simplicity, craftsmanship, and "dignity of effort." Modern golf architecture is undergoing a shift toward the values that made the classic courses worth restoring: the love of crafting features by hand. But it's also frustrating for golf architects to take time to craft something if they know that unregulated technology will render the design features obsolete in 5 years.

There is a reason people travel from all over the world to play the two (and soon, three) courses at the Bandon Dunes resort in Oregon, crafted in the spirit of Arts and Crafts ideals. Sure, it has modern amenities and golfers still bring their high-tech clubs along for the trip, but the attention to design detail, the journey to get there, and the overall atmosphere is authentic and reassuring.

The enthusiasm for Bandon Dunes has inspired a new level of passion among those who work there, those who maintain their finished designs, and most of all, the golfers who play there.

REASSESSING OUR GOLFING VALUES

"The furor which golf is creating at the moment among all classes seems all the more extraordinary when one recalls that less than thirty years ago the game was looked upon as something effeminate—an unmanly sport suited only to the pink-coated fops and dandies who played it."
                                                    —ROBERT HUNTER, 1926

Like most other first-time visitors to San Francisco Golf Club, our group got lost looking for the hard-to-find entrance. When we finally did pull into a small asphalt area, devoid of any white stripes to tell us where to park, we assumed (correctly as it turned out), that this was the main parking lot. To make things more confusing, the first tee and pro shop were within just a few feet of the lot. When we found our way into the dark, musty locker room, the old metal lockers were stacked with shoes and umbrellas trying to dry out.

We finally found the locker room attendant. Old enough to have ushered at Ford's Theater the night Lincoln was shot, he sat behind a desk, sound asleep. It was eight in the morning.

"Well," we thought, "this is an interesting start." Four hours later after playing one of the world's most fascinating designs, the "experience" took on charm like no other in golf. The corresponding low-profile maintenance of both the Old World design and the facilities gave San Francisco Golf Club an unforgettable character.

Some new golfers, raised on corporate golf facilities seemingly born out of the Courtyard by Marriott manual, would have trouble appreciating an experience so unconventional. I'll never forget it.

Modern golfers have little problem believing that an old club can get away with such odd encounters. Rarely do they see that a timeless, character-rich golf course makes up for any perceived imperfections.

Few clubs or courses built in the last 10 years have been able to adopt this old-style simplicity—the kind that emphasizes the character of the golf over the amenities. It should make sense to emphasize the course (where you spend 4 to 5 hours) over the clubhouse (usually less than an hour).

Modern golf all too often assumed that "high-end" values are vital to success and compensate for any flaws in the golf course. The focus on everything but the character of course design has sent the sport on a rendezvous with economic failure.

The values of modern golf revolve around luxury clubhouses, manicured turf, lavish aesthetics, a costly and shallow obsession with "branding," and an inability to take advantage of technology to build better, less expensive courses. Instead, courses are built like four-star hotels, which are dazzling on first arrival, but annoying on repeat visits when you know where to go and just want to get out on the links to find some peace and quiet.

Garish design features that look expensive and photograph well for the advertising brochures rarely hold up on repeat visits. All too often we see *virtual* golf—which offers little substance or value for the customer who seeks an authentic golfing experience.

WHY SPORTY GOLF MATTERS

Golf evolved into a sport because, like fishing or hunting, it provided a battle against nature (minus the bloodshed, usually). Golf was played amid natural settings and no one dreamed of complaining about unfair bounces, brown spots in the fairway, unrepaired divots, passing beverage carts, blind shots, the occasional wandering sheep, or the green's proximity to a town road. Any such interferences were part of doing battle with the elements, part of the adventure.

At St. Andrews, there was no out-of-bounds along the eighteenth hole until the last few decades, so it was not uncommon to see a golfer playing off the steps of a building next to the home hole.

We will never get back to the purest forms of nineteenth-century "native golf," nor do we need to. But understanding that a spirit of adventure was present when golf began will help us restore certain traditions and values that most golfers still yearn for, even if they don't know it.

WHAT IS BEAUTIFUL?

Modern golf has fallen in love with pretty. "Orchestrating Color" was recently a magazine cover story for the biggest golf superintendent's publication. Ornamental trees, cascading waterfalls accented by bronze statues, and bunker sand visible from outer space are employed at ridiculous expense.

Are we designing golf courses or producing lavish Broadway musicals?

Do we want to be in nature or in an outdoor amusement park?

Consider this silliness. A half-million cubic yards of dirt, considered a "minimalist" earthmoving effort, is shifted into containment mounds so golfers can see the entire hole and be treated more fairly. Such mounds are like those inflatable bumpers put in the bowling alley gutters so the five year olds won't bowl gutter balls.

You have to ask, what's the point of even teeing off if design will kick most of the balls back to the center?

We also see millions of cubic yards of dirt shifted so golfers don't have to see something egregious like a road or a row of homes. It's the same road they drove on to reach the course, and the same homes they live in.

The "pretty" that golf has embraced is entirely cosmetic. Beauty is no longer nature-based. Irregularly shaped lines, soft hues, and native plant material are not considered beautiful by most, yet the most famous courses are beloved for their very use of the materials at hand.

Nope! Man stamping his imprint on the land and cleaning things up, now that's pretty! And expensive. And at times, offensive.

TECHNOLOGY MANAGEMENT

If golf is going to maintain its popularity and an economic future, it must examine the incredible technology and information it has been handed by many intelligent folks. Instead of viewing technology as a way of reducing the time or work necessary to get a job done while allowing for a greater profit margin, technology must be applied to make golf courses easier to maintain and safer for the environment. That's happening. Golf courses have never been better conditioned in the history of the sport.

Because of the impact technology has made (and will continue to make thanks to hawkish companies and USGA incompetence), courses are too long and won't be getting any shorter. Remember the rubber band. It's stretching and narrowing, and soon it will snap.

Regulation is purported to be un-American and antibusiness, yet how many deregulated industries like the airlines, cable television, and energy sectors really benefit their customers when regulation is trashed? Rules are in place not only to regulate business but also to secure that business. Regulated industries that see their rules circumvented (like commercial fishing) ultimately suffer.

CONSIDER SWEDEN

It costs less than the equivalent of $2,000 to join top clubs, and annual dues are a few hundred dollars in Sweden. Greens fees top out at $50 and often are less than half that. And when golfers pay less, the overall atmosphere is more relaxed.

More importantly, Sweden has learned from the Scottish golf model by embracing *familiesport*—golf as a family sport. Clubs encourage junior members. Of the 600,000 golfers in Sweden, 90,000 are juniors! Course memberships for kids cost about $25, including lessons. Pros get $125 from a foundation for each child that they teach regularly.

Clubs, individuals, and the government all emphasize community. The goal is to make people feel welcome and to keep things relaxed and fun. Recreational benefits come first; the economic opportunities come second.

Because Swedes have refused the fast food, mass production, and brand-name addictions that have *not* worked for the American golf business—and embraced the creative side of the game—golf is thriving in Sweden.

THE FUTURE OF GOLF

Golf's future is far from certain, but it can thrive again with a more balanced approach to architecture, technology, maintenance, and courses. It is even possible that affordable and fun golf could play an integral role in rejuvenating the spirit of community that so many Americans long for.

It will take an awakened golfing public and help from the professional ranks to support the USGA in taking proper care of the sport, assuming the USGA is motivated to take action. Their inability to communicate a message has been further undermined by their actions.

Our classic courses must be allowed to survive as intriguing tests of golf, not thrown into the trash heap of history or stretched into corrupted versions of their former glory. In order to save the courses and the sport, someone must regulate the golf ball, and preferably for both professional and everyday golf.

More important than the change in distance, improved golf ball regulation would take back some of the control equipment makers now have over golf. Manufacturers have shown that they do not deserve to dictate the sport as their interests have nothing to do with golf's long-term needs.

If the USGA chooses not to protect golf and its future, they may face a challenge from a prestigious course or organization that is willing to provide leadership by introducing their own set of simplified, understandable rules and their own golf ball specifications. The USGA might even be surprised to know that some of their longtime admirers already have floated this idea. With the Internet and alternative handicapping services available, such a revolution would be surprisingly simple.

Who is going to step forward? When and how?

I don't know. But it had better be soon.

EPILOGUE

ALIGNING STARS

"In no other sport are the equipment manufacturers so influential when it comes to how the game is played. Spalding and Nike don't control basketball. But the equipment companies in golf have enormous sway via advertising and sponsorship dollars, and they are the chief obstacle to reform."

—SALLY JENKINS, *WASHINGTON POST*, JULY 2004

A "devil's advocate" friend admitted that he has been transformed into an addicted consumer, unable to resist the latest "thing" to get a little more distance or accuracy off the tee.

Even though he openly despises the notion that he is a consumer first and golfer second, he reasons that most golfers are the same: The lure of a few more yards is just too tempting.

For him, the cost of this temptation typically means shelling out $300 on eBay for a used or soon-to-be-discontinued driver. Others are less discerning and pay much more just to keep up.

So I posed a scenario using his home course, an affordable daily-fee layout that offers a good value and interesting design elements.

Using one of the holes as an example, I explained how the architects had created a parallel hole situation that was becoming unsafe, due to either (A) the majority of average golfers becoming "better athletes," or (B) new distance advances thanks to hot balls and optimized launch conditions (a more likely scenario).

When this particular course was built a few years ago, the architects assumed that a majority of golfers teeing off on one hole could not reach golfers standing on an adjoining tee. But with the latest unregulated ball-driver combination, now even my friend can slice a tee shot onto that adjoining tee.

Inevitably, someone will get hit by an incoming tee shot and an insurance company will pay out a small or large sum depending on the injuries incurred. The insurance company will eventually raise their rates when more incidents occur in places once deemed safe.

That increased premium gets passed along to the golfer. Now, my friend is willing to pay for the latest driver, but the idea of paying a higher green fee that goes straight to an insurance company isn't very attractive. Neither is the idea that the course becomes a less safe place for the mingling golfer to stand, especially as rounds take longer.

He still insisted that the temptation was too great, so I asked him if he was starting out as a golfer today, would he even bother? Not at these prices, no.

Scenarios such as the safety issue and many others involving slow play and higher costs can only continue to evolve out of the mess created by deregulation of golf equipment. So, whether the issues raised in this book make you want to laugh or cry, any observer has to be encouraged by various developments outlined in these pages and in the following updates.

The stars have aligned to take the game back from corporateers. Tiger Woods, Arnold Palmer, Jack Nicklaus, and the folks in Augusta, Georgia, have stated their cases for change, as have many other famous players and noted writers.

Even two of the four major equipment corporations—Callaway and Nike—appear ready to sign off on a competition ball concept that will drastically change corporate America's influence on the sport. Perhaps they finally realized that they will thrive financially if the game flourishes on all levels.

Who will step up and set the dominoes in motion? The USGA? The Royal and Ancient Golf Club of St. Andrews? Hootie Johnson? Wally Uihlein and Titleist?

The following recent developments answer some of these questions.

AUGUSTA NATIONAL FED UP?

An anonymous club official told *Golf World*'s Ron Sirak in the April 16, 2004, issue: "The club wants to identify a threshold for distance that, when reached, would trigger a rollback in how far the ball goes. While the club would prefer that the USGA and the R&A take the lead, it would also not hesitate to act unilaterally to protect its course."

"The club will be proactive in protecting the course," said another source. In 2005, Augusta National will allow the PGA Tour to employ its ShotLink technology to measure driving distance and clubs used for approach shots on all the holes because the club is "concerned not just with the fact that tee shots are going 320 yards but also that seven-irons are going 190 yards. Flying the ball high into these greens neutralizes one of the course's main defenses."

Augusta National Chairman Hootie Johnson's 2004 Masters press conference yielded this exchange, where it was obvious Johnson understood the distance issue better than his questioner.

> **Q**: Any more thought about the golf ball issue and going with a standardized, for lack of a better term, Masters ball, or is the golf course big enough that you don't have to worry about that for a while?

> **Hootie Johnson**: Well, we worry about it, but we are glad that the governing bodies do have a plan, and hopefully that will take care of it. I have to say that it does concern me that we are starting at 320 yards, and if we have any slippage and it takes any length of time to correct any violation of that, it will be at a point where I think it will be damaging to the game. You look like I didn't make myself clear, and I may not have.

> **Q**: You said 320 yards. I'm not sure what that was a reference to.

> **Hootie Johnson**: I believe that that is public; that the USGA and the R&A are together on 320 yards, and I think we have this equipment and the clubhead speed would be at 120 miles an hour. I think I'm right on this. And I'm just saying that we are starting at a level, at a pretty high level, distance.

Hootie Johnson can't be happy that he has spent millions changing the course for the "next generation" of players, only to have the current generation already catch up in just 2 years.

Later in the summer, former USGA president and masters championship committee chair Will Nicholson spoke to the *Denver Post*.

"The ball is destroying a lot of the great, traditional golf courses in this country, and I think it's a crime," Nicholson said. "I think if there's a consensus among the governing bodies—the USGA, the PGA Tour, the LPGA, the European—all the tours and all the marquee players, those are customers. The manufacturers have to do what the customer wants, and if the customer wants a ball that doesn't go as far, I think they'll adjust to it appropriately."

Furthermore, Nicholson said, "I don't think it's going to affect the great majority of players if you do it right."

Since Nicholson likely does not speak out on such weighty issues without first making sure he's on the same page as Augusta National chairman Hootie Johnson, his comments suggest that the club is moving closer to adopting its own ball specifications.

CALLAWAY'S SPEEDY OBSOLESCENCE

The Golf Channel's Adam Barr offered an in-depth look at the recent financial struggles of Callaway and the resignation of CEO Ron Drapeau.

"In Callaway's June earnings revision and throughout the industry," writes Barr, "experts echoed concern over at least 2 years of downward price pressure on metal woods as a reason for sluggish revenue streams."

The most interesting and funny tidbit (as long as you are not a Callaway shareholder) involved the manufacturers super-rapid product turnover and the impact this race to the bottom, er, top, is having on companies like Callaway.

Golf pros report that many golfers are growing weary of feeling like they have to keep up with the latest driver. Other golfers can't afford to keep up with say, Taylor Made's new $799 R7 driver (screwdriver kit included), so they feel left behind.

The rapid nature of innovation is not only driving people from the game and hurting the pocketbooks of customers who can't say no to the latest driver, but also undermining the business plan of companies pushing products a bit too rapidly.

"The concomitant pressure to innovate faster and faster, repeatedly recapturing the consumer imagination while not angering buyers with computer industry–style speedy obsolescence, makes golf one of the most difficult subsegments in the leisure products market," Barr writes. "And faster (read: more expensive) innovation leads to more late-model closeouts and—you guessed it—more downward price pressure."

So the golf equipment industry is now moving from the already insidious Wall Street driven concept of "planned obsolescence" (they don't make 'em like they used to), to a cycle that calls on rapid innovation and flashy marketing designed to make the golfer feel as if they are using obsolete equipment if they haven't picked up this month's driver.

But the cycles move so fast that the companies are no longer able to exploit the suggested retail price long enough to produce expected earnings.

Where can we send donations?

HANNIGAN CONTINUES
TO MAKE THE CASE

Former USGA executive director Frank Hannigan, writing for the excellent *Golfobserver.com*, continued to offer fresh insights on the distance debate:

> Think of it this way: Billy Mayfair, who has not worn out any treadmills or Stairmasters, is 4 yards longer than Jack Nicklaus was in his prime.
>
> The USGA pretends that a rollback is a technical problem on the order of sending a manned spacecraft to Mars. Actually, a rollback is a legal and political problem. The USGA, even though it has more money than Croesus, has been unwilling to take any act that might invite litigation. A rollback in distance would spur a lawsuit.
>
> The USGA is also afraid to do anything that might get anybody mad. The average golfer gets nothing out of the new equipment but thinks he does. There is a theory that this 17-handicapper would revolt against the USGA. A very high-paid crisis manager was brought in by the USGA in 1998. She counseled them not to do anything to inflame their constituents. The USGA Executive Committee took her advice. Some governing body!
>
> Tim Finchem and his policy board do not want a competition ball which might expose them in an anti-trust case as a co-conspirator. A competition ball might also lead to the loss of endorsement money. Why would Acushnet want to pay Davis Love $4.5 million a year to endorse a ball he can't even use? The whole thing is a mess.

TOUR PLAYERS SPEAK OUT

You don't often read comments from golf professionals about the state of the game because many are paid six- and seven-digit salaries to endorse manufacturer products.

However, several players just couldn't hold back any longer.

Nick Price, January 2004: "The equipment has made a lot of mediocre players good players. Your best players will always rise to the top irrespective of what equipment they use—but it is the middle pack. There is a very fine line in this sport. The difference between a guy who is going to shoot 15- or 16-under and the guy who shoots 8-under is small. If you have equipment to help you and give you the edge it makes it easier. Hitting nine-iron second shots into par 5s is really hurting the game. I'm worried that golf will end up like tennis, where it is all about power and not finesse."

Tom Weiskopf, July 2004: "Didn't they slow the ball down at Wimbledon? That was for a reason. They wanted to improve the rallies. They wanted to protect the game of tennis. There should be a tournament ball in golf, but the USGA and the R&A have turned their backs on their responsibilities."

Seve Ballesteros, *Golfweek*, February 12, 2004: "We are getting close to just tee it up and push a button and just talk to the club and say, 'Hey, I want a left-to-right,' and it will react. I would make the ball bigger, which would be nice for some people who are erratic off the tee. It would be easy to find the ball and it will stop the ball from going so far."

Mike Clayton, after Ernie Els shoots 12-under par 60 at Royal Melbourne in February 2004: "The amateur bodies in Britain and America have the power to alter the ball, but they are reluctant to do so for three reasons. The first is they are afraid of lawsuits from the makers. The second is the average amateur has benefited little despite what they would like to believe, and the third is there is more than a hint the amateur bodies do not think there is even a problem. Unless something is done to reduce the distance the ball flies, the legislators are treating the legacy of designers such as Mackenzie with contempt. It is time someone stood up to the manufacturing lobby and made it clear who runs the game."

Steve Flesch, *Golfweek*, March 5, 2004: "There isn't any imagination in the game anymore."

Paul McGinley, discussing the changes in the style of game now being played on the professional tours, *Golf World*, February 28, 2004: "I am fortunate I can now hit the ball a long way. I wouldn't like to be a young guy coming on the tour who only hits it 250 to 260 yards off the tee. He has virtually no chance. The Corey Pavins of the game are gone."

Arnold Palmer, *Desert Sun*, February 15, 2004: "At some point, if you continue to design a golf course to accommodate the way they hit the ball today, you are just going to run out of land. You are just going to have nothing but big, long golf holes, and I wouldn't enjoy playing any of them."

Jack Nicklaus: "It's absurd. You have to restrict the ball. The game gets ruined. It makes absolutely no sense whatsoever to allow the golf ball to do what it is doing."

Arnold Palmer, at the 2004 Masters: "If you don't slow it down, as time goes on, the problem is going to become more severe."

Mickey Wright, *Palm Beach Post*, February 2004: "It's amazing to me that a 64-year-old man like Jack Nicklaus can hit it three clubs farther than in his prime."

Jack Nicklaus, at his 2004 Masters press conference: "I build them, and as soon as I give them to the owner I say they are obsolete. [Press laughs.] And they are. I mean, every time you start a golf course, it takes you a couple of years to do it. By the time you've gone through 2 years to change the golf course, they have changed the equipment enough that you haven't designed for it."

And then Nicklaus told the assembled journalists, "You don't want me on that today."

Bob Tway, July 2004: "It's past the point where enough is enough. Maybe I'm a little bit old school but I think something definitely needs to be done. A lot of these golf courses don't have room to keep moving the tees back."

Gary Player, July 2004: "Right now, right at this moment, in any golf tournament, there's no such thing as a par 5. No such thing for the regular (tour) guys. Every time they tee it up now, it's a par 68. There's no such thing as a par 72, it's a par 68."

Gary Player, August 2004: "Golf is in a very serious predicament at the moment professional-wise. Leave equipment as it is for amateurs, but the R&A (Royal & Ancient Golf Club of St. Andrews) and the USGA (U.S. Golf Association), they still don't get it. They don't realize what's happening in golf. As we sit here, there are people sitting in their little factories and big factories and trying to make the ball go farther and trying to come out with a new driver. I believe there are a lot of golfers today that are playing golf with drivers that are not 100 percent legal. How are you going to tell them? Cut it open? Try it, you'll get sued. I see guys out here [on the Champions Tour] now hitting the ball over 300 yards. They couldn't do that when they were young men . . . at the prime of their strength. So I don't know where we're going."

Phil Mickelson, July 2004: "In the future, we'll see length be more of a factor. I just don't see the courses continuing to be capped like this off the tee. I think we will start playing longer courses, because as distances have increased over 10 percent, that has not happened to the golf courses. A 7,000-yard golf course would have to be 7,700 yards [today] to be what it was years ago."

TAKE DEANE BEMAN OFF THE USGA CHRISTMAS CARD LIST

"There is not strong enough leadership to bring perspective," former PGA Tour commissioner Deane Beman said of the USGA in a July 2004 *Golf World* feature.

Beman pointed out that at the USGA, "there is a great tendency for no one to be responsible. [The USGA's] role is to preserve and protect, not to preserve and protect [its] treasure. They either think what is happening now is right, or they don't think they have the authority, or they are afraid of losing money. I maintain the money the USGA has is not worth a nickel if they don't use it to protect the game. Better that they should get in a lawsuit and lose it all than to allow ourselves to go where we are going."

For Beman, playing with the current generation of balls, with their improved aerodynamics, is akin to using the smaller 1.62-inch-diameter ball formerly played outside the United States.

"The modern ball plays better [easier] than the 1.62 ball used to, the one that required less skill," Beman said. "So from a skill level, we've gone backward. Real ball-striking ability that comes with playing unforgiving equipment is going backward. The players aren't as good as they could be if they played less forgiving equipment. And I think it takes away from golf."

Beman says the USGA is "responsible for where we are, and they won't own up to it." Beman says he is most concerned with mandating balls curve more, that are more vulnerable to the side spin imparted by a miss-struck shot and less impervious to the wind. It would "still be possible for somebody who is bigger and stronger to play better," he says. "It just gets rid of the free pass."

NOTED COLUMNIST SAYS "THEY JUST WANT TO MOVE PRODUCT"

Washington Post columnist Sally Jenkins wrote a July 2004 column headlined, "Destruction of Golf in Progress."

> You can be anti-technology when it comes to golf, without being one of those uncompromising purists who thinks we should go back to hickory shafts. Which of us doesn't long for the days when a par 4 was supposed to be played . . . in four strokes? Now, thanks to megabrute drivers designed to maximize something called the "co-efficient of restitution," and jumped-up balls made with the aid of computer launch monitors, a par on the PGA Tour is 2½ strokes. Spin rates have taken some of the "sport" out of the sport, and made it a little less human and revealing.
>
> The real problem with golf is not science itself, but that it's been ap-plied to the game so rampantly by equipment companies interested only in selling the "newest" clubs and balls for even higher prices. They don't care if Augusta is stretched to the point of ruin, or if a 480-yard hole has to be turned into a par 4. They just want to move product. In no other sport are the equipment manufacturers so influential when it comes to how the game is played. Spalding and Nike don't control basketball. But the equipment companies in golf have enormous sway via advertis-ing and sponsorship dollars, and they are the chief obstacle to reform.

R&A FEELS NO SENSE OF
URGENCY ON EQUIPMENT ISSUE

Helping to settle the question of who will not be stepping up to the plate is Peter Dawson, secretary of the Royal and Ancient Golf Club of St. Andrews.

Following a stellar 2004 British Open where the smartest, grittiest, and most imaginative player came out on top (Todd Hamilton), Dawson talked to reporters and ignited a long overdue debate over whether the merely great professional players were catching up to the world's best, thanks largely to technology.

Mike Aiken wrote in the *Scotsman*, "Tiger Woods and Ernie Els, by far the best golfers on the planet with eleven major titles between them, are among those who have expressed their reservations to Peter Dawson, the secretary of the Royal and Ancient, about the impact big-headed drivers and multilayered balls are having at the highest echelons of the game."

According to Dawson, leading players have (finally) noticed that the impact of new technology has become a problem. Regrettably, they may be pointing to Hamilton's win as the sign that "anyone" can now win a major. That's not fair since Hamilton was ranked among the top sixty players in the world. Either way, the top players have noticed their advantage has been diminished by equipment technology.

Dawson said that even though new technology may "have a slight bearing" on the outcome of the Open, "it's not a question of urgency."

A few weeks later, the *Scotsman's* John Huggan wrote about Hamilton's win and the demise of the driver in championship golf:

> In the last six holes Hamilton played before he lifted the Claret Jug skyward, he used what used to be a wooden club only once; and that was to chip stiff from just short of the final green. While the fairways were not so narrow that he couldn't sensibly have hit a driver from the tees, Hamilton—unlike Ernie Els—chose not to. And won.
>
> The problem, however, is not that Hamilton won; or that he defeated a supposedly superior player in the four-hole play-off; or that he chose to hit irons; it is that he could play so safe and then still be able to hit relatively short irons to the greens. How boring is that?

TIGER WOODS TAKES A STAND

Alright, a lot has happened. The point has been made. But all of these events are relatively minor compared with the most powerful figure in modern golf taking a stand on the distance issue.

Responding to a question about Peter Dawson's comments, Tiger Woods said, "I've spoken to Peter Dawson on that subject saying that we should all be playing under the same rules. We shouldn't have the auspices of the R&A and the USGA being conflicted. We shouldn't have amateur golf and professional golf being under two different scenarios, two different rules. I think it would be great for all of golf to be played under the same umbrella, the same rules. That's why we changed from the small ball to the same uniform-size golf ball. I think we should all be playing under the same rules, not just under different auspices depending on where you are around the world."

Then Woods explained what he would do to deal with the distance issue.

"I think you should put a limit on the speed of a golf ball, the spin rate of a golf ball. You can increase the spin of the golf ball and make it so that we don't hit the ball as far. You can decrease the speed of the core. There's different ways you can get around it so that we're all playing under certain speed limits. Hopefully that will be the answer to a lot of the problems that we're having with golf course design around the world."

A week later at the choreographed prime-time "Battle at the Bridges," Woods was asked by Andy North to clarify his comments on the distance issue. Woods reiterated the above remarks, again suggesting that the spin rate of the ball be increased to reduce distance flight and perhaps even to return the art of shaping shots. Woods also said that something needs to be done because "we're starting to realize that we're running out of property on a lot of these great golf courses."

Because Woods said this during a "slump," many were quick to write off the comments, if they saw the barely reported comments at all. But anyone who has followed the sport in recent years knew it was only a matter of time before Tiger would recognize that the strengths of his game—creativity, imagination, and natural power—became less of an advantage for him as technology evolved.

Woods likely made these comments with the OK of his most prominent sponsor and burgeoning ball manufacturer, Nike. This means the Oregon-based megacorporation has either seen the light or simply wants to undercut rival Titleist.

Either way, Tiger's concept is valid. It would eliminate the complexities inherent in the "competition ball" concept, which bifurcates the sport and would likely affect only golfers on the higher end of the swing-speed spectrum.

However, such a modification would require the USGA to act and develop a test to enforce an altered spin rate. This would require that the USGA admit its previous "optimization" test was sound, while its revitalized Iron Byron is useless.

Woods has given the governing bodies a place to begin a discussion that desperately needs to take place in a public forum. Though Woods has much in common with golfing legends Bobby Jones and Jack Nicklaus, he now shares another view that those two greats held in their playing prime: Control distance to end the distance race. Even though there are many different views about how to accomplish change, a consensus is building that something must be done.

An end to the distance chase stops the madness of golf existing primarily as a consumption pastime revolving around the marketing and quarterly profit margin needs of a few manufacturers obligated to no one but their stockholders.

Shifting the focus back to the sport itself will benefit the shareholders who matter most: golfers.

Don't worry, manufacturers. Golfers will continue to buy new clubs regardless of their "coefficient of restitution." And they'll always need a fresh sleeve of balls, regardless of their spin rate.

APPENDIX

PEOPLE DOING GREAT THINGS

Please go to *www.geoffshackelford.com* and check out the page devoted to *The Future of Golf*. I want to hear about innovative golf professionals, superintendents, managers, companies, and golfers who are giving back to the sport—say, folks who have created successful junior or beginner programs, or creative types who've managed to make a course work well on a tiny budget. And we need to hear more about courses that support caddies, PGA Tour hopefuls, or golf societies that legitimately protect important golfing traditions.

WEB SITES WORTH BOOKMARKING

www.golfclubatlas.com—In-depth reviews of course designs with photos and reader course comments. Also, a lively discussion of courses and issues in the sport monitored by industry heavyweights.

www.pasturegolf.com—A site devoted to low-cost, nature-inspired golf: "We are the ones moved by the fact that Bobby Jones would not recognize the Augusta course he loved if he saw it today. We are the ones who are tired of the trend of manicured courses, high-priced greens fees, and the insult of super technological golf clubs and balls that lower your score while stealing away the essence of the game along with your life savings."

www.golfobserver.com—Daily summary of golf writing with exclusive commentaries and discussion group.

www.accessgolf.org—Interesting initiative to promote golf as a rehabilitation tool for those with disabilities.

www.antiqueclubs.org—Jeff Ellis's devotion to golf's early, handcrafted works of art.

www.golfcollectors.com—Society devoted to preserving, collecting, and celebrating tradition.

www.usga.org—Web site for the governing body of golf includes the rules of golf, annual reports, press releases, green section articles, and news on USGA championships.

www.ngcoa.org—National Golf Course Owners Association Web site where you can read about several interesting initiatives and programs designed for beginners and junior golfers. "Kids on the Course" appears to be the most promising.

www.thegolfchannel.com—Well-organized and frequently updated site for news and the occasional commentary worth reading.

www.linksmagazine.com—Many articles from this fine magazine are posted here.

www.golfdigest.com—Updated daily, including content not published in the magazines. *Golf World* magazine can be found here as can most *Golf Digest* features, including many excellent in-depth interviews with golf dignitaries.

www.golfonline.com—*Golf Magazine*'s online site includes Web-exclusive columns from David Feherty and major championship coverage not found in the magazine.

www.golfweek.com—Less content but still worth a look now and then to see what the "Forecaddie" has to say.

sportsillustrated.cnn.com/golf/—*Sports Illustrated*'s excellent Web-exclusive coverage includes insights from SI writers and the opportunity to email questions to their golf reporters.

www.pga.com—Industry news and everything wonderful you need to know about the PGA of America.

www.pgatour.com—Includes the once-excellent "Golfweb" archives—if you look long and hard and want to remember how interesting Internet content used to be.

www.lpga.com—For those who follow the LPGA Tour, this is a little more lively than the PGA Tour's site.

www.geoffshackelford.com—The author's site.

WHEN AND WHERE SELECTED ESSAYS FIRST APPEARED

The following articles and columns previously appeared in other publications, though most have since been updated and edited to suit the content of this book. They are reprinted here with permission.

Part I—What's Up with Golf . . . in a Big Nutshell
Golf Was a Sport—*Golfdom Magazine*, May 2003

Part II—Technology
They Said It, Not Me—*Golfdom*, October 2003

Part III—Major Identity Crisis
Out of Sync: The Grand Slam—*Golf Magazine*, August 2003
(appeared as "Major Identity Crisis")
Where Risk Is No Longer Rewarding—*Los Angeles Times*,
April 10, 2003
The Bunker, R.I.P.—*Golfdom*, November 2000
The (Lost?) Art of Course Setup—*Links Magazine*, May/June 2003
More Progress: Slow Play—*Golfdom*, August 2004
To Bifurcate or Not to Bifurcate—*Los Angeles Times*, February 25,
2003 (appeared as "A New Driving Range Beyond
the Average Golfer")

Part V—Driving Up Cost, Driving Down Golf
MBA Golf—*Golfdom*, August 2002
Why Can't They Build Them Like They Used To?—*Senior Golfer*,
January 2001 (appeared as "Trick or Treat?")

Why Can't They Name Them Like They Used To?—
Golfdom, September 2004
The Politics of Design—*Golfdom*, October 2001
The Reality of Rankings—*Golfdom*, January 2000
What's in a Signature?—*Golfdom*, September 2001
Y7K?—*Golfdom*, July 2000
Blinding!—*Golfdom*, March 2000
Small Greens Are Overrated—*Golfdom*, September 2002
A Thing Unto Itself—*Golfdom*, February 2001

Part VI—Restoring Golf's Character
The Case for the Classic Course Ball—*Golfdom*, October 2003
Theme Courses: Kitsch or Fun?—*Golfdom*, November 2001
A Think Tank . . . That Thinks—*Golfdom*, November 2003
Restore Classic Muni's—*Golf World*, July 12, 2002
Go Native—*Golfdom*, November 2003
The Art that Is Life—*Golfdom*, May 2001
Reassessing Our Golfing Values—*Golfdom*, January 2002

ABOUT THE AUTHOR

GEOFF SHACKELFORD is the author of eight previous books on golf. His writings have appeared in *Links*, *Golf*, *Golf World*, *Golf Digest*, the *Los Angeles Times*, the *Masters Journal*, *golfobserver.com*, and *Golfdom*.

He is the co-architect with Gil Hanse and Jim Wagner of Rustic Canyon Golf Course in Moorpark, California—Golf Digest's "Best New Affordable Public Course in America" of 2002.

Geoff played collegiate golf at Pepperdine and has taught a Harvard University seminar on golf course restoration. He resides in Santa Monica, California, and can be contacted through his Web site, *www.geoff shackelford.com*.